The Best Of
The Mailbox®

Learning Centers
Preschool/Kindergarten

Editor In Chief:
Marge Michel

Product Director:
Kathy Wolf

Editors:
Ada Hanley Goren
Sharon Murphy
Laurel Robinson

Artists:
Jennifer T. Bennett
Cathy Spangler Bruce
Clevell Harris
Donna K. Teal

Cover Design:
Jim Counts

About This Book

The Best Of The Mailbox® *Learning Centers* for Preschool/Kindergarten is a collection of the best learning centers published in the Preschool/Kindergarten editions of *The Mailbox*® from 1988 to 1994. It is designed to provide an extensive collection of skill-specific, teacher-created, easy-to-make learning centers for today's busy teacher. Each learning center includes an illustration and complete instructions, as well as any necessary reproducible patterns.

www.themailbox.com

©1996 by THE EDUCATION CENTER, INC.
All rights reserved.
ISBN# 1-56234-149-9

Manufactured in the United States
10 9 8 7 6 5 4

Table Of Contents

FINE-MOTOR SKILLS

Fish Food

Do your youngsters wiggle away whenever you try to involve them in cutting practice? Then prepare to reel them in, with this "feed the fish" activity. To make a fish, duplicate two copies of the fish pattern (page 67) on bright tagboard. Laminate, cut out, and glue or staple the two fish designs together, leaving a large opening at the fish's mouth. Suspend several fish at children's eye levels, if desired, so that the fish seem to "swim" through the air. Provide construction-paper scraps and scissors. Visitors to this center cut wiggly worms from the paper scraps and "feed" them to the fish.

To convert this center for any type of matching practice, program each fish using a permanent marker. Then program laminated, 1 1/2" circles cut from ultralucent gift wrap to correspond to the programming on each fish. To match, a student puts the bubbles in the fish mouths. Another student removes them to check.

Karen Tonkin
Creekside Washington Elementary
Creekside, PA

Nuts!

Help refine those fine-motor muscles with this nutty activity! Place a pair of tongs in a basket of unshelled mixed nuts. Place that basket in another similar-sized basket. To use this center, separate the baskets and challenge a youngster to transfer all of the nuts from one basket to the other using only the tongs!

Bobbie Hallman—Gr. K
Burbank School
Merced, CA

A Stretchy Board

This hands-on activity will help stretch your youngsters' imaginations and help develop small-muscle control. In advance, paint or stain an 8" x 10" piece of wood. Every few inches, hammer a 2 1/2-inch nail into the wood, leaving about two inches of the nail exposed. Place the board in a center along with rubber bands of different colors and sizes. To use this center, a child places a rubber band around a nail and stretches it to one or more nails. Have him continue in this manner, until he makes a design that's to his liking.

Tonie Liddle—Pre/K
Central Baptist Christian Academy
Binghamton, NY

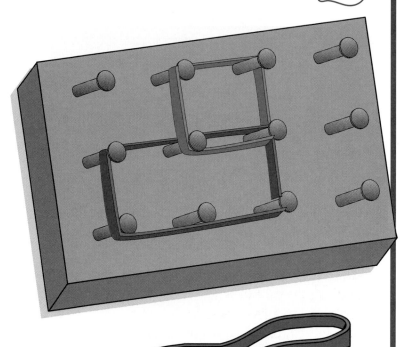

Nuts And Bolts

There'll be a whole lot of twisting and turning taking place at this fine-motor skill center. Purchase an assortment of different-sized nut-and-bolt sets from a hardware store. Place the separated pieces in a decorated container at a center. A student matches each nut to its corresponding bolt, then screws the nut in place. After all the nuts and bolts have been paired, he unscrews the pieces before replacing them in the container. Now that's a task for busy little fingers!

Tanya Wheeler—Gr. K
Pelahatchie Elementary
Pelahatchie, MS

FINE-MOTOR SKILLS

Pipe Works

Try this direct pipeline to hand-eye coordination and fine-motor skill development. Provide approximately 40 pieces of 1/2" PVC pipe, twenty 1/2" connectors, and fifteen 1/2" T-joints. Youngsters twist, turn, and connect the hardware to create unique pipe systems.

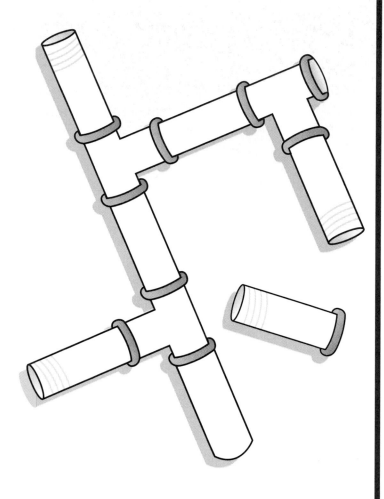

Big Blocks

Liven up your block center with these attractive, lightweight building blocks. Collect a supply of concentrated detergent boxes. Tape over the opening of each box with packaging tape. Cover each box with adhesive covering. Youngsters will demonstrate new realms of creativity when they're building with these larger-than-life blocks!

Mary Maurer
Children's Corner
Durant, OK

Block Shop

Youngsters will love this center since it offers them an opportunity to do work usually reserved for grown-ups. And you'll love this center since it offers an unusual way for students to practice fine- and gross-motor skills. Stock the center with a large box containing pieces of scrap wood, a large empty box (for holding the sanded wood), and several small sheets of sandpaper. To use the center, each participant takes a piece of wood from the box and sands it until it's smooth enough to be used in the block corner. When he's done, he places the block in the other box. Periodically, check the box of sanded wood for pieces that are smooth enough to be moved to the block area. Return all other pieces to the original box for more sanding.

Kim Bohl
Blissfield, MI

Holiday Lacing Cards

Recycle old holiday cards into inexpensive lacing cards. Keeping a holiday card closed, punch evenly spaced holes along all four outer edges. To make a lace, dip one end of a two-foot yarn length in glue. When the glue has hardened, tie the other end of the yarn length through a pair of holes. At a center, place a supply of lacing cards (prepared for lacing) in a holiday gift box. A youngster selects a card, then laces it on all four sides. When the lacing is complete, assist each youngster in tying off and trimming the loose end of the lace. Completed projects can be displayed on the classroom tree or in windowsills.

Lynn Bowling—Preschool
Decatur First United Methodist Kindergarten
Decatur, GA

FINE-MOTOR SKILLS

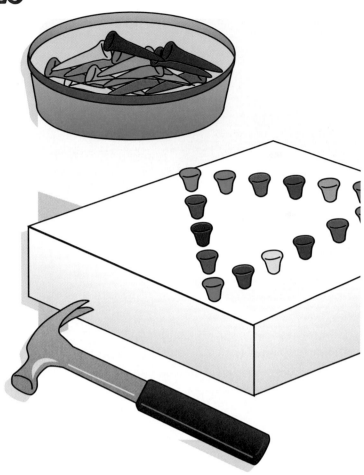

Quiet Hammering

Here's a chance to provide youngsters with some motivating eye-hand coordination practice—without a lot of noise! Use reusable adhesive to attach a thick Styrofoam® sheet to the top of a woodworking table. Provide lots of colorful golf tees and a hammer or two. Your youngsters will have fun creating shapes, patterns, designs, and number sets by hammering the golf tees into the Styrofoam®.

Diane Bonica
Tigard-Tualatin School District
Tualatin, OR

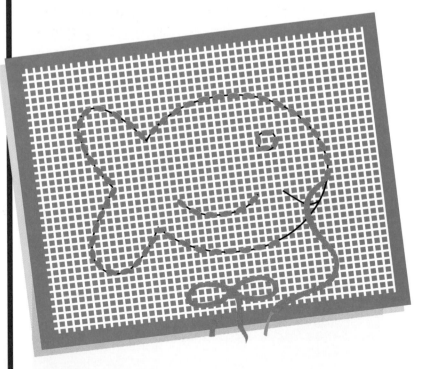

"Sew" Much Fun!

Your students will enjoy sewing works of art with this activity. Using a permanent marker, draw shapes, letters, numbers, or designs on pieces of plastic canvas. (Plastic canvas is used for needlepoint work and is available at craft stores.) Also provide some blank plastic-canvas pieces for original creations. Tie a long length of yarn to each canvas piece. Wrap a piece of tape around the loose end of each yarn length to form a needle. Place all of the supplies in a center or housekeeping area. To do this activity, a child sews along one of the design outlines or sews an original needlepoint creation.

Jeanne Taylor—Pre/K
Cincinnati, OH

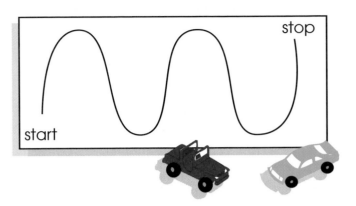

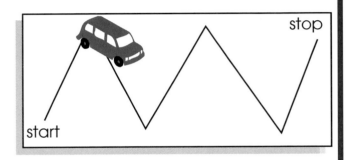

On The Road
To Fine-Motor Coordination

Cut a poster board into four strips for these fine-motor practice activities disguised as racetracks. Draw a different "road" on each strip, and write "start" on the left and "stop" on the right. Provide four, small plastic cars. Children "drive" on the roads from left to right.

Nancy Farlow—Gr. K
St. Joseph, MO

A "Hole" Lot Of Fun!

Promote small-motor coordination at this fun-filled center. Place a paper punch, a cake pan, a large Ziploc® bag, and several construction-paper strips at the center. A student makes a collection of confetti by holding a construction-paper strip over the cake pan and punching a series of holes in the strip. He then carefully deposits his confetti in the Ziploc® bag. For added pleasure, coordinate the color of the confetti to the current season or holiday. Fall confetti could be red, yellow, orange, and brown, while Halloween confetti could be black and orange. Use the confetti later to embellish seasonal art projects.

Kim Bohl
Blissfield Elementary School
Blissfield, MI

Keys To My Heart

Melt youngsters' hearts with this tactile matching center. Collect various shapes and sizes of old keys; then program red poster-board heart cutouts by tracing each key on a cutout. Laminate the cutouts and store them along with the keys, in a pencil box which has been decorated to resemble a valentine treasure chest. To use this center, students match keys to their outlines on the heart cutouts.

Barbara Boldt—Gr. K
St. Luke's Episcopal School
Watauga, TX

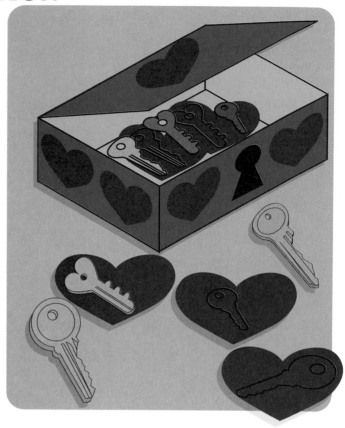

Find The Outline

Make this matching center in a snap! On a large piece of poster board, trace the outlines of several differently shaped objects. Laminate the poster board for durability. Store the traced objects in a container at the center. Students place each object atop its matching outline.

Becki Bolm—Grs. K-1
Bowmar Avenue School
Vicksburg, MS

Book-Order Concentration

Don't throw away those extra book club order forms! Recycle them into appealing Concentration-style games. Cut out the pictures of the books featured in two identical order forms. Pair matching pictures and glue each one onto a poster-board square. Laminate the squares for durability and store them in a Ziploc® bag. To play, a youngster turns all of the squares facedown on a tabletop. He then turns over two squares. If the pictures match, he removes them and sets them aside. If they do not match, he turns them over again and takes another turn. Play continues until all pairs are matched. To vary the activity, have youngsters play in pairs or in small groups.

Karen Martin—Gr. K
Hahira Elementary School
Hahira, GA

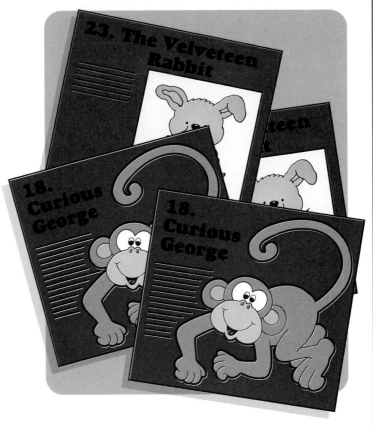

Fabric Sample Cards

Challenge and maintain your little ones' visual-discrimination skills with this easy-to-make matching center. To make this center, use samples found in wallpaper books or fabric sample books. Cut a variety of equal-sized samples. Cut some samples of identical patterns in different color schemes and some samples that would be appropriate for matching pattern halves. Mount each sample on a construction-paper card. Make a puzzle-style cut in each of the cards that you intend to use for matching halves, but leave the cards for matching identical patterns of different color schemes whole. Display the cards all together or according to their attributes, depending on your youngsters' ability levels. To do this activity, a child matches the whole cards by pattern and/or matches each puzzle piece to its mate.

Mary Maurer
Children's Corner
Durant, OK

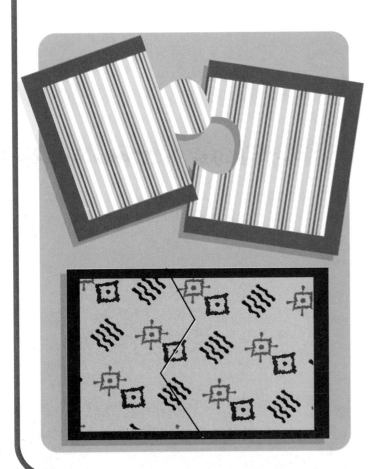

What's The Clue?

Verbal clues provide the missing links at this center. Mount five pictures of common objects onto five pieces of tagboard. Code the back of each picture with two differently colored stickers, one sticker on each half. Laminate the pictures; then cut them in half, making certain that each picture half is identifiable and bears a sticker. Store the pieces in a container at the center. To play, two students sort the pieces (according to sticker colors) between them. Each student holds his pieces so only he can view the pictures. In turn, each student gives a clue describing a picture on one of his pieces. The other student shows a piece he thinks will complete the picture. Play continues until all pictures have been matched.

Teddy Bear Twins

As students practice visual-discrimination skills they help little bears find their twins! Duplicate the bear pattern (page 68) on construction paper. Using the clothing patterns (page 69 and 70) as tracers, cut a set of clothing from each of several wallpaper samples. Mount the clothing cutouts atop the bear patterns. Code the backs of twin bears for self-checking; then laminate and cut out the dressed bears. Store the cutouts in a Ziploc® bag at the center. Students pair twin bears by matching those wearing clothing of the same designs.

Nancy Farlow—Pre-K/Kindergarten
St. Joseph, MO

Pumpkin Patch Matches

Peek at this pumpkin patch for an easy-to-make visual discrimination activity. Use the patterns on page 71 to make two sets of matching jack-o'-lantern faces. Glue one set of shapes inside a file folder and add pumpkin patch details. Store the second set of shapes in a pocket attached to the back of the folder. Students sort the shapes by matching the pumpkin faces. Laminate the folder and pieces for durability.

Barbara Boldt—Gr. K
Children's World Learning Center
Bedford, TX

Spooky Match

A Spooky Match

Make this matching activity in minutes! Varying the order, place the same five patterns from page 72 down each side of a piece of poster board. Insert a brad near the inside edge of each pattern. Tie yarn lengths around the brads on the left. Children wrap the yarn lengths around the brads of matching pictures on the right. Make a new center for each holiday or season by using seasonal stickers!

Nancy Farlow
St. Joseph, MO

A Bunch Of Balloons

Choose several brightly colored wallpaper patterns to make this visual-discrimination center. Cut two balloon shapes from each pattern. Glue one balloon from each pattern onto a large piece of poster board and laminate. Children match remaining balloon patterns to the poster.

Tammy Kohlenberg—Gr. K
Duson Elementary School
Youngsville, LA

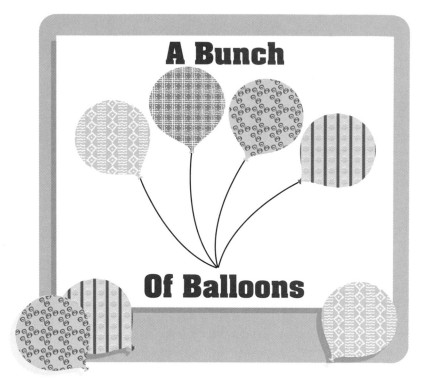

Jelly Bean Jubilee

Sweeten up visual-discrimination skills with this jazzy jelly-bean jar. Repeatedly trace a three-inch oval (jelly bean) pattern onto a large poster-board jar cutout. Trace and cut out a matching number of white construction-paper jelly beans. Using colored markers, decorate the jar as desired and program each jelly-bean cutout with a different pattern. Cut each decorated cutout in half; then glue one half of each cutout atop a different oval on the jar cutout. Laminate for durability; then store the halves of the jelly-bean cutouts in a jelly-bean bag. Attach a bunny cutout to the back of the jar if desired. A youngster draws a jelly-bean half from the bag, then places it beside its matching half on the jar. Successful matchers will jump for joy when rewarded with a handful of jelly beans!

ISUAL DISCRIMINATION

Turkey Shape Match

a gobblin' good shape-matching ac-
a large sheet of poster board, paste
from page 73 with quite a bit of
etween them (see the illustration). For
ape, make an identical shape cutout.
one side of a small piece of Velcro® to
of the poster-board turkeys and the
side of the Velcro® to each of the shape
uts. To do this activity, a youngster
tches each shape cutout to the turkey with
e same-shape body, then sticks the two
des of Velcro® together.

Beth Taylor Devlin—Pre-K Special Education
Dutch Lane Elementary School
Hicksville, NY

Velcro®

Magnetic
tape

"Magic" Matching

This matching activity will draw your
students like a magnet. You'll need a metal
pan, some magnetic tape, and two copies
of page 74—one duplicated on colored
construction paper and the other on white
copy paper. Cut out the shapes from the
colored copy, back them with poster
board, and laminate them. Attach magnetic tape to each piece. Store the magnetic pieces in a Ziploc® bag. Program the
pan by taping the white copy inside. Students can now magically match the
shapes. Try this with any cut-and-paste
worksheet.

Sandra Posey—Pre/K
Juan Seguin Elementary School
Canyon Lake, TX

Button-Up Shapes

Matching shapes takes on a new dimension in this durable center. Machine stitch around an 8" x 36" piece of burlap. Cut two sets of identical felt shapes before arranging and sewing one set onto the burlap. Then sew a button in the center of each of these shapes. In the center of the remaining shapes, run fabric glue lines. These lines should be a little longer than the diameters of the buttons on the other shapes. Allow to dry overnight. Use scissors to cut through the center of the glue line on each felt shape. To use this center, students "button" each shape onto the corresponding shape on the burlap background.

Dawn Hurley—Gr. K
Asbury Kindergarten
Columbia, SC

A Box Of Chocolates

Use a heart-shaped box of chocolates for a sweet review of shapes. Remove the chocolates from the candy divider. Using markers or shape stickers, label each section of the divider or each even interval of the box bottom with a shape(s). In the same manner, program the bottoms of chocolate kisses with shapes to match those in the candy box. Place the chocolates in a resealable plastic bag. Place the bag and the empty candy box in a center with a bowl of chocolate kisses. To use this center, a child takes each piece of chocolate from the bag and places it on the corresponding shape in the box. After all of the chocolates have been placed, allow the youngster to enjoy a chocolate kiss from the bowl.

adapted from an idea by Dawn Spurck—Director
Creative Play Center
Colorado Springs, CO

Holiday Puzzlers

Challenge thinking skills with holiday puzzles. To make a puzzle, lay six to eight Popsicle® sticks side by side; then add a strip of masking tape to hold them together. Flip over the set of sticks; then use permanent markers to program the sticks with a holiday drawing and, if desired, the corresponding word. Remove the tape from the sticks, and store the sticks in a holiday gift bag. Place several bags in a holiday gift box at a center. A youngster selects a bag, removes the sticks, and places them faceup on a tabletop. He then arranges the sticks to create a holiday picture.

Jeanine Davy—Gr. K
Immaculate Conception School
Lake Charles, LA

Notepad Puzzles

All the pieces come together with this unique puzzle center. Collect interesting die-cut notepad sheets; then laminate them. Cut the shapes into puzzle pieces, varying the number of pieces to match the abilities of your students. Then place each set of pieces in a separate plastic bag. Put the bags in a center randomly or according to theme. To use this center, a child takes one bag and puts the puzzle pieces together.

Penni Flood—Pre/K
Park Village Elementary
San Antonio, TX

MAKING ASSOCIATIONS

Inside/Outside

Classifying everyday activities is the focus of this center. Program the inside of a file folder as shown. Program a set of index cards with pictures of activities which take place inside and outside. Code the back of each card with an illustration of a house (inside) or sun (outside) for self-checking. Laminate the folder and the cards for durability. Attach a Press-on Pocket (available from The Education Center, Inc.) to each side of the folder. Store the cards in the pockets when not in use. To use this center, a youngster removes the cards from the pockets, shuffles them, and places each card in the correct pocket. When all cards have been placed in a pocket, he removes them one at a time, flipping each one over to check.

Nancy Dunaway
Forrest City, AR

Go-Togethers

Work on a youngster's pairing ability while strengthening that all-important tripod grasp as well! You will need a supply of spring-type clothespins and an even number of poster-board cards. Glue animal pictures on half of the cards; then glue pictures of animal homes on the rest of the cards. Have youngsters pair animals with their homes; then use a clothespin to clip each of the pairs together. Adapt this center for additional pairing practice with go-together nouns (bat/ball etc.), rhyming pictures, or opposite pictures.

Nursery Rhyme Matchups

Put children's love for nursery rhymes to good use. Cut out nursery rhyme pictures from a coloring book or storybook. Glue pairs of related pictures (wall/Humpty Dumpty, Little Miss Muffet/spider, etc.) on poster-board strips; then laminate. Cut each strip in half, varying the cuts. Students find the matching pieces and fit them together. This activity is self-checking since only related pictures will fit together. Place the pieces in a box decorated with nursery rhyme stickers.

Kathleen Geddes Darby—Gr. K
Garvin School
Cumberland, RI

Critter Capers

Pair up animal-shaped cutouts with matching skills for critter capers your youngsters will love! From light brown construction paper or tagboard, cut two each of several animal shapes that are found in a box of animal crackers. Place the cutouts in an empty animal cracker box. A youngster removes the cutouts from the box, spreads them out on a tabletop, and pairs each cutout with its match. For a special treat, allow each successful matcher to munch a few animal crackers. Here come the animals, two by two!

Liz Mooney—Gr. K
Central Rayne School
Rayne, LA

GOLDEN, CRISPY, DELICIOUS

Animal Crackers

Stir It Up

Stir up color skills with a collection of paint-stirring sticks from local paint stores. Paint the end of each stick a different color. (If you have enough sticks, paint several sticks of each color.) Store all of the sticks in a paint can. For each color of stick, wrap a matching color of construction paper around a can. (Depending on your youngsters' skill levels, you might label each of the cans with only a color word.) Have a youngster match colors by putting each paint stick in the appropriate can.

Karen D. Turner—Gr. K
Red Boiling Springs School
Red Boiling Springs, TN

Colorful Gumballs

Colorful gumballs fill this center with matching fun. Use the pattern on page 75 to make a large gumball machine cutout. Add details with markers or paint. Program the cutout with four-inch circles featuring different color words. Cut out a four-inch construction-paper circle to match each of the colors programmed on the cutout. Laminate the pieces for durability. Using self-adhesive Velcro®, attach each colored gumball cutout to the matching circle on the gumball machine. A student removes all of the gumball cutouts, then reattaches them to the corresponding color words. Reward successful color matchers with a penny to use in the classroom gumball machine.

Kris Young—Gr. K
Toth Elementary School
Perrysburg, OH

Button Sorting

Fill a sock with buttons that have two, four, or zero holes in them. On each of three pieces of tagboard (sized to fit inside the sock), draw a button to represent each category of button in the sock. Store all of the supplies in the sock. Have a youngster empty the sock and sort the buttons according to the number of holes.

Debbie Johannsen—Gr. K
John Glenn School
Donahue, IA

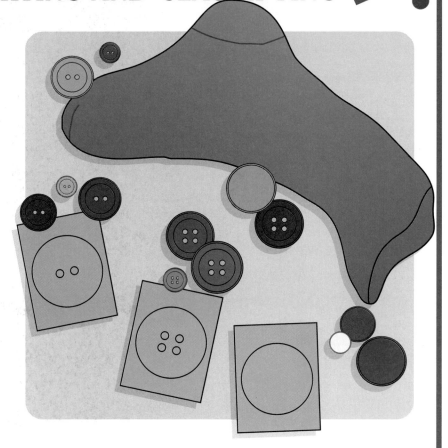

Lost—And Found!

Your school's lost-and-found may be just what you need to create this interesting sorting center. Rummage through your school's lost-and-found box in search of unclaimed hair accessories. Wash the hair accessories, including barrettes, ribbons, and bows. Store them in a decorated hatbox; then place the box in a center. To use this center, a child sorts the hair accessories by color, size, or design. Vary this activity by having youngsters make patterns using the hair accessories.

Melinda S. Edwards—Pre/K
Northside Elementary
Rock Hill, SC

SORTING AND CLASSIFYING

Let's Do The Laundry

Take advantage of the fact that little ones often jump at the chance to do grown-up chores! Stock a laundry basket with sock pairs in a variety of colors, sizes, textures, and designs. Place a container of clothespins in the laundry basket. Tape a length of rope to a nearby wall. Have a youngster pin the socks to the rope according to a given attribute. For example, you might ask a youngster to sort and pin the socks according to color, size, texture, or design.

Debra L. Dechaine—Pre-K
Terryville, CT

Place "Mat-nipulatives"

Create an assortment of colorful, durable "mat-nipulatives" from vinyl placemats. Cut old vinyl placemats into different shapes of varying sizes. Place the shapes in a decorated container at a center. Youngsters can classify the shapes by color, size, or shape or use them as counters. For added fun, attach a strip of magnetic tape to the back of each shape and allow youngsters to manipulate the shapes on the chalkboard or other magnetic surface.

Pat Bollinger—Gr. K
Leopold R-3
Leopold, MO

Yes/No Box

Here's an easy-to-make, versatile center no classroom should be without. Staple together two identical boxes. Program one box "yes" and the other "no." Program a card with a question such as "Is it red?" or "Does it start with an s?" Place an assortment of items or pictures of items (some having the attribute and some not) in a small container. To use this center, a youngster selects an item or picture from the container, determines whether or not it has the attribute, then places it in the appropriate box. With very little effort, a new center can be created for almost any skill.

Vicki Sherman—Gr. K
Central Elementary School
Centerville, IA

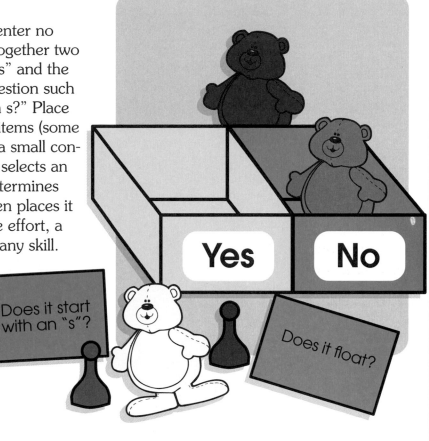

Batter Up!

Capitalize on your youngsters' natural fascination with baseball cards by using them in a learning center! Collect a supply of baseball cards and put them in a shoebox from a pair of athletic shoes. Have youngsters sort the cards according to teams or positions played.

Pat Bollinger—Gr. K
Leopold R-3
Leopold, MO

SORTING AND CLASSIFYING

Sizing It Up

Practice size seriation with a bunch of fun stuff! Collect and label small, medium, and large laundry detergent boxes. Also collect items that come in small, medium, and large sizes such as toothpaste boxes, glue bottles, plastic eggs, bubble bottles, buttons, and tinfoil pans. Store the mediuma nd small box and all of the items for sorting in the large box. Have a youngster empty the contents of the large box and sort them according to size. Now that's just about the size of it!

Kaye Sowell—Gr. K
Pelahatchie Elementary School
Pelahatchie, MS

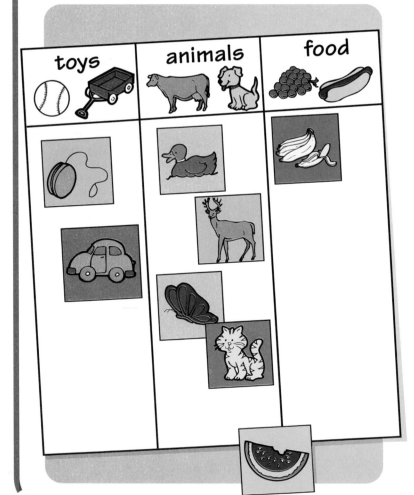

Classification Station

Youngsters' classifying abilities will be enhanced when they get a chance to sort it all out! Divide a sheet of poster board into three equal sections. Label and illustrate each section with a category such as "toys," "animals," or "food." Cut several pictures from magazines or old workbooks to represent each of the categories. Mount the pictures on construction-paper squares; then laminate the pictures and the poster board. (For picture storage, attach a Press-On Pocket to the back of the poster board.) For a classifying activity, a youngster places the pictures on the board under the appropriate category. Make additional "Classification Stations," varying the level of difficulty according to your youngsters' needs.

Santa's Back!

What could be more fun that sorting Santa's sack? Draw four large rectangles on the inside of a green file folder. Label the rectangles "toys," "tools," "pets," and "clothing." Divide each rectangle into fourths, and cut 16 matching shapes from red construction paper. Cut and mount appropriate pictures for sorting (four for each category) on the construction-paper cutouts. Program the backs of the cutouts for self-checking. Decorate the outside of the folder with the pattern on page 87, then laminate the folder and pieces for durability. Store the pieces in a Press-On Pocket attached to the back of the folder. Students rush to Santa's rescue, sort his sack, and send him on his way to visit the good little boys and girls!

Elizabeth Harris—ESL Teacher
Kimball Elementary School
Mesquite, TX

Seasonal Matchups

Here's a center for all seasons! Divide a colorful file folder into four sections. Program each section with a different symbol to represent "winter," "spring," "summer," or "fall." Glue seasonal pictures (3–4 for each season) atop 3" x 5" index cards. Program the back of each card with the matching seasonal symbol for self-checking; then laminate the cards if desired. Store the cards in a Press-on Pocket attached to the back of the folder. To use this activity, a child matches the pictures to the appropriate sections of the folder, then flips over each card to check.

Nancy Dunaway
Forrest City, AR

It's News To Me!

Make headlines with this fun letter-recognition center! Each week, display one page from a newspaper in a center. Post an oversized class roster nearby, along with a letter cutout representing the letter that you wish students to search for. In turn, each student visits the center and counts the number of times he sees the specified letter on the newspaper page. The child writes (or dictates) the numeral next to his name on the class roster. At the end of the week, work as a large group to identify and circle the letter each time it appears on the newspaper page. Then count the number of appearances to find out who had the most accurate answer.

Peggy Marcel—Gr. K
Acadian Elementary
Houma, LA

Lots And Lots Of Letters

For each child, trace a giant version of the letter of the week on a sheet of construction paper. Place the papers in a center, along with a supply of old magazines and newspapers. As each child visits the center, have her cut out one copy of the letter and label it with her name. Then instruct her to search through the magazines and newspapers and cut out as many printed versions of the letter as possible. Have her glue the cutout letters to her giant letter. Vary this activity by having youngsters search for pictures that have the letter's beginning sound instead of or in addition to the letter cutouts.

Janet Paczak—Gr. K
Stevens Elementary
Brandon, MS

Letter Lacers

Letter recognition was never "sew" easy for students! Using a permanent marker, program Styrofoam® plates with upper- and lowercase letters. Punch evenly spaced holes through the letter outlines on the plates with golf tees. For a tactile letter-recognition activity, have students use brightly colored shoestrings to lace the letters.

Sandra Hatton—Gr. K
Garth Elementary School
Georgetown, KY

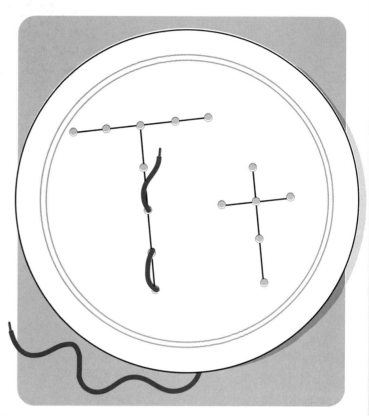

Sponge Letter Matching

Soften your approach to letter recognition with sponge letters. On a separate poster-board square, trace around each letter in a set of sponge letters. Store the squares and matching sponge letters in a large Ziploc® bag. To begin, select a few squares and matching sponge letters, and place them in a box at a center. A youngster places each letter on its matching outline. As youngsters begin to soak up letter-recognition skills, add different or additional squares and letters to the box.

Wendy Titus
Timberlake Christian School
Lynchburg, VA

Mama And Me

This center will be a surefire hit! Duplicate several copies of the patterns on page 76 on yellow construction paper. Color the ducks with markers. Label each mother duck with an uppercase letter and each duckling with a matching lowercase letter; then laminate and cut out the ducks. Students "reunite" each duckling with its matching mother. To make a pocket for storage, staple the sides of a brightly colored file folder. Glue a copy of each pattern to the front and add the title. Store the center pieces inside.

Tommie Netzer
Teacher's Tools
Hurst, TX

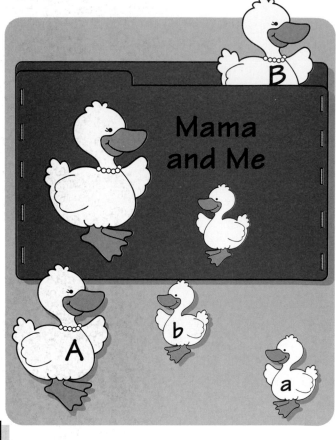

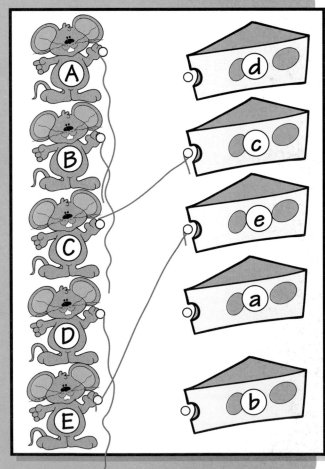

Going For The Cheese!

Students join mice and cheese cutouts by matching upper- and lowercase letters at this center. Using the patterns on page 77, cut and color a matching number of construction-paper mice and cheese cutouts. Label each pair with matching upper- and lowercase letters. Attach the cutouts to poster board as shown and laminate; then insert a brad to the inside edge of each cutout as shown. Attach yarn lengths to the brads next to the mice. The child connects each yarn length to the brad next to the matching cheese cutout. You can count on these mice being well fed!

The Friendly Ghost Castle

Youngsters will be eager to see who or what lurks behind each door in this friendly fortress. To make the center, duplicate the haunted house on page 78 and two copies of the ghost patterns on page 79. Laminate them if desired. Cut out each ghost pattern and cut on the dotted lines around the door and windows of the haunted house. Mount the haunted house on a sheet of tagboard and decorate the rest of the sheet as desired, or have student helpers do it. Label the door and each of the windows with an uppercase letter. For each door and window, program two of the ghost patterns with the same matching lowercase letter. Behind the door and each of the windows, glue a ghost that is labeled with that matching letter. Store the remaining ghosts in a zippered plastic bag. To use this center, a child removes the ghosts from the bag, matches each ghost to a window or door, and then opens the door or window to check her work.

adapted from an idea by Liz Herwig—Pre-K
Sanlando Christian School
Longwood, FL

Please, Feed the Monkey

Youngsters will be climbing the tree of letter recognition after monkeying around at this center for a while. Enlarge and duplicate the monkey pattern on page 80 onto construction paper. For each letter that you wish to study, duplicate the banana patterns on page 81 onto construction paper. Color and cut out the patterns and mount only the monkey cutout on poster board; then laminate all of the cutouts. Cut an opening for the monkey's mouth; then glue the monkey cutout onto a block of wood that will enable it to "stand" upright. Program half of the supply of banana cutouts with uppercase letters and the other half with lowercase letters. A youngster places the banana cutouts faceup on a table, then matches an uppercase letter to a lowercase letter. When he has found a match, a youngster "feeds" the matched bananas to the monkey. Change skills on the bananas by wiping off the original programming with a spritz of hair spray.

Sheila Sorrell—Gr. K
Mallory Elementary
Mallory, WV

Flip The Lid

To preview the formations of lowercase letters, use caps from plastic milk jugs. Print an uppercase letter on the top of each lid. On the inside of the lid, print the matching lowercase letter. Have a student select five caps and lay them on a table with the uppercase letters showing. He then copies each uppercase letter and prints the corresponding lowercase letter beside it. To check, he flips the cap. Ask your students or cafeteria staff to save caps for you. Store the caps in a half-gallon milk carton.

Barbara Boldt—Gr. K
Children's World
Bedford, TX

Heart To Heart

Label the left sides of several heart cutouts (made from the pattern on page 82) with uppercase letters. Program the right side of each cutout with the matching lowercase letter and two additional lowercase distractors. Punch a hole to the right of each lowercase letter. Program the cutouts on the backs for self-checking; then laminate. Tape a yarn length to the back of each cutout behind the uppercase letter. Seal the remaining yarn ends with tape for easy threading. Students thread the lengths of yarn through the holes on the right side of the cutouts to indicate the matching lowercase letters, then turn over the cutouts to check their work.

D. Jean Busby
Caldwell, AR

Mother And Child

These pouches are packed with learning possibilities! For each letter that you wish to include, duplicate the mama and baby kangaroo patterns (page 83) onto tagboard. Color and cut out the patterns. (After cutting out the mama kangaroo patterns, make additional cuts along the lines representing her forelegs.) Slip a library card pocket under the forelegs on each mama kangaroo; then glue the pockets in place. Laminate the patterns; then program each of the mama and baby kangaroos with an uppercase or lowercase letter, respectively. Make a slit along each library card pocket's opening. To use this center, a child matches a baby to a mama kangaroo, then slides the baby into the mama's pouch.

Julia Elsen—Preschool
Thatcher, AZ

Catch 'n' Match

"Take down your fishing pole and meet me at the fishing hole!" To stock a fishbowl, make a tracer from the fish pattern on page 83; then trace and cut out 26 tagboard fish. Label each fish with a different uppercase letter; then slide a paper clip onto each fish. Store the fish in a fishbowl. To make a pond, trace and cut out 26 construction-paper fish. Glue these fish onto a large sheet of construction paper (or several sheets taped together). Label each fish with a different lowercase letter. To make a fishing pole, tie a length of string onto the end of a wooden dowel; then attach a magnet to the other end of the string.

Have a child fish around in the fishbowl until he catches a fish, then match that fish to a fish in the pond that bears the lowercase letter match. Continue fishing until all the fish have a match.

Linda Sauer—Preschool
Teddy Bear Hugs Nursery School
Webster, NY

Pick-A-Pocket

Here's a prime place to reinforce beginning-letter sounds. To prepare the center, attach three fabric pockets to a poster board as shown. Label each pocket with a different letter. Then, for each letter, cut out several magazine pictures with the same beginning sound. Back each picture with a piece of construction paper; then glue each picture to the end of a craft stick. To use the center, students place each picture in the appropriate pocket.

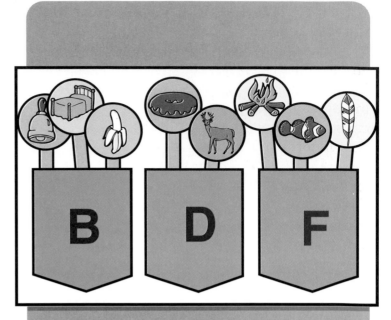

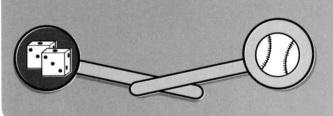

Shape Pads

Use colorful shape notepads to make this versatile seasonal center. To make this center, cut out the picture discs on page 84. Glue each of the discs onto a separate page from a seasonal shape notepad. Label additional pages with corresponding letters of the alphabet. Laminate and cut out all the pages. Program a page from the notepad with directions for the center; then glue that page to the front of a string-tie envelope. Store all the pages in the envelope.

To use this center, a child matches a letter page to a picture page according to the picture's beginning sound. As an added challenge, a child puts all the pages in alphabetical order.

adapted from an idea by Pat Biancardi—T-K–1
Homan School
Schererville, IN

Letter Munchers

These gobbling guys provide a novel way to reinforce beginning sounds and recycle empty tissue boxes. To make a Letter Muncher, stand a tissue box on end. Using the open area as an open mouth, glue a construction-paper face and features to the box. If necessary, cut the box to extend the mouth area. Label the Muncher with the letter of your choice. To prepare the munchies, glue—or have children glue—cut-out magazine pictures to pieces of construction paper. (The mounted pictures must be small enough to fit through the mouth area.) To use this center, a child looks at each picture and determines whether or not it begins with the indicated letter. If it does, he feeds it to the Letter Muncher. If it doesn't, he sets it aside.

Cathie Pesa
P.C. Bunn Elementary
Youngstown, OH

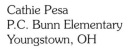

A Pretty Poinsettia

A pretty poinsettia takes shape as beginning consonant letters and sounds are matched. Use the patterns on page 85 to make this center. Trace the cutouts onto poster board in the configuration of a poinsettia flower. Add details to complete the flower using colored markers. Label the petals of the flower with beginning consonants; then label matching petal cutouts with corresponding pictures. Students place the petal cutouts on the poster board by matching the pictures to their beginning consonants.

Kathleen Darby
Cumberland, RI

Strings Attached

Youngsters will get to pull a few strings at this center! Divide a sheet of poster board into sections as shown. In each section, glue a magazine or workbook picture in the middle. Then attach a blank seasonal sticker to each side of the section. Program one of the stickers with the correct beginning letter for the picture and the other with an incorrect letter choice. Next to each sticker, cut a small slit (about 1/2 inch) in the board. On the back of the board, program a smiling face (or other symbol cue) behind each picture's correct beginning letter. Poke a brad through the lower portion of the center of each section. Securely tie a piece of yarn around the head of each brad; then secure the brad to the board. To use this center, a child looks at a picture, then slides the yarn into the slit next to the sticker with the beginning letter for that picture. To check his work, the child simply turns over the board and looks for a smiling face by each strand of yarn. If a smiling face does not appear on that side, he turns over the board and looks at the picture again, then corrects his work.

Tops Galore

Spinning around looking for center ideas? This one is just tops! Save colored tops from milk and juice jugs. Place a blank sticker label on each of the tops. Program each of a set of tops with the skill of your choice to coincide with a programmed file folder. For example, program a file folder with pictures and coinciding spaces in which to place the tops. Program each of a set of tops with a beginning consonant to match a picture on the folder. A youngster matches the letter on a top with a picture by placing a top in the space nearest the picture. An endless variety of manipulative file-folder centers can be made with tops!

Betty L. Gomillion—Gr. K
South Leake Elementary
Walnut Grove, MS

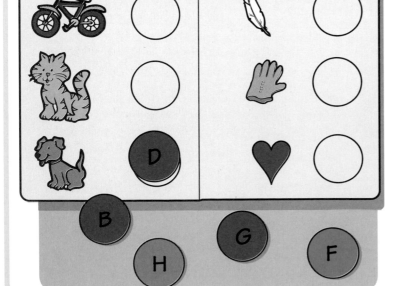

ABC Treasure

Enlist the help of youngsters and their families to make this center, and before you know it, you've got something to explore! Label each of 26 strawberry baskets with a letter of the alphabet. Stack the baskets in a large Rubbermaid® treasure chest. Over a period of time, collect small items to put in the letter baskets such as a Band-Aid®, windup penguin, or toy eggbeater. When each of the baskets has at least one item in it, put the treasure chest in a center. To use the center, a youngster or small group of youngsters may alphabetize the baskets or pour out all of the treasures and replace them in the appropriate letter baskets. For an added challenge, provide a graph with a row for each letter of the alphabet (or use only certain letters). At various times during the year, have youngsters graph the number of treasures beginning with each letter.

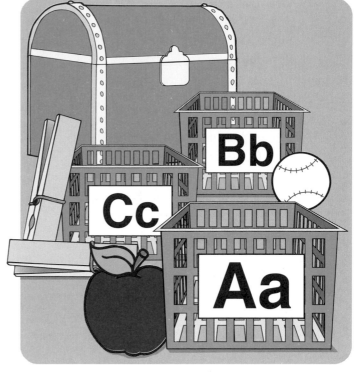

Betty Lynn Scholtz—Gr. K
St. Ann's Catholic School
Charlotte, NC

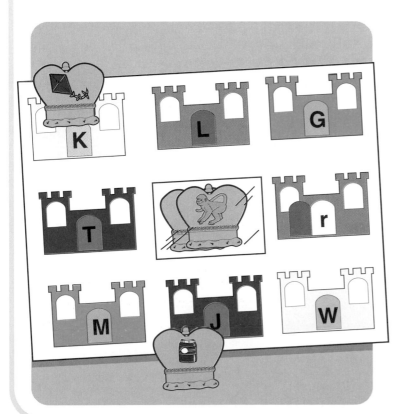

Crowns And Castles

Practice initial-consonant sounds in a royal way! Duplicate the crown and castle patterns on page 86 onto different colors of construction paper. Cut slits around the top, right, and bottom sides of the castle doors before cutting out the castles and crowns. Decorate the crowns with glitter and sequins, if desired. Glue the castles onto a large sheet of poster board, leaving the door unglued. Program a different uppercase letter on the outside of each castle door. Open each door to write the matching lowercase letter behind it. On each crown, glue a picture that corresponds to the programming on a castle door. If desired, program a lowercase answer on the back of each crown for self-checking. Have a child match the picture on a crown to the castle with the correct beginning letter. Where is your home, your majesty?

Karen Jackson—Gr. K
Vina Kindergarten
Vina, AL

Spell It!

This hands-on activity will help your emergent readers learn to spell familiar words. To make the center, locate stickers or pictures of common words and glue them to the inside of a file folder. Next to each picture, trace wooden or plastic letters to spell the word. Laminate the folder. Place the folder and a supply of letters in a center. As each child visits the center, she can match the block letters to the outlined letters. You'll soon have super spellers!

Wendy Darcy—Gr. K
Northside Elementary
Hitchcock, TX

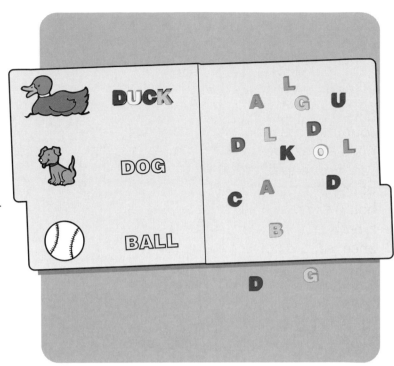

Colorful Color Words

Color words take shape at this colorful center. From tagboard of corresponding colors, trace and cut out the letters of several color words. Place the cutouts in a large Ziploc® bag at the center. A student first sorts the letters by color, then arranges each set of letter cutouts to spell the matching color word. Display a poster of corresponding color words to aid students with spelling if desired. There you have it! A colorful color and color-word recognition center!

Taryn Grinker—Gr. K
Vine Elementary
Cincinnati, OH

Alphabet Soup

Warm up to name recognition and spelling with a bowl of alphabet soup. To make the center, paint the middle of a paper plate red to represent the soup. Decorate a large sheet of construction paper or poster board to resemble a placemat (or use a real one). To complete the ambiance, set the bowl of soup, a napkin, and a plastic spoon on the placemat next to a supply of uncooked alphabet pasta. A youngster searches through the pasta to find the letters of his name and "floats" them in order on top of the soup. Soup's on!

Carol Aitken
Tampa, FL

Alphabet Stew

Warm up emergent reading skills with a big pot of alphabet stew. Label a supply of Ping-Pong® balls with one letter each. Put all the balls in a large pot. Place the pot, a soup bowl, and a large ladle or scoop at a center. To use this center, a child scoops a ladle full of stew (Ping-Pong® balls) into the bowl, then names the letter on each of the balls. Vary this activity by having a youngster alphabetize the letters he has scooped out or name something that begins with each letter's sound. Some youngsters might even spell familiar words. (If you need to keep the Ping-Pong® balls from rolling away, have youngsters manipulate the Ping-Pong® balls on a small, decorative dish towel.)

Writing Temptations

Create interest with a touch of variety to motivate your youngsters to spend time in your classroom writing center. Choose from the following supplies to provide youngsters with new and unique experiences in the world of print: gold, bronze, and silver crayons; assorted colors of paper (including black); feathers and paint; scented markers; all colors of chalk; chalkboards; a typewriter; letter stamps; colored pencils; a tray with salt (to "write" with fingertips); envelopes; adding-machine tape; order forms; and waitress tablets. Extra! Extra! *Write* all about it!

Paula Laughtland—Preschool
Bright & Early Primary School
Edmonds, WA

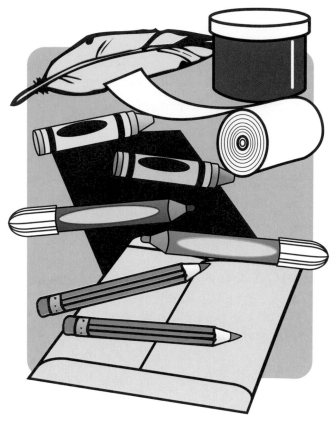

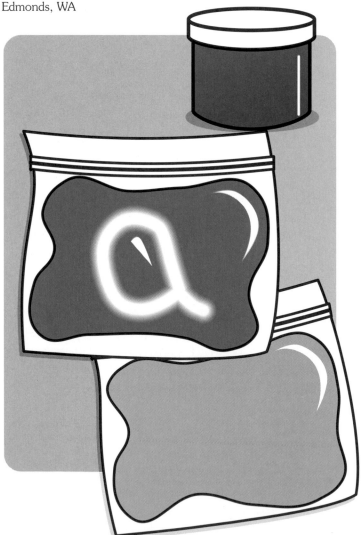

Zippy Writing Practice

For a tactile, colorful, squishy-fun approach to letter writing, put a different color of finger paint into each of several large Ziploc® bags. Close the bag securely before spreading out the paint in each of the bags. Children can use their fingers to practice random strokes or writing letters. To erase, a child simply rubs his hand over the bag and he's ready to start again.

Jeanette Warwick—Pre-K
Berkley/Campostella Early Childhood Center
Norfolk, VA

Special Delivery!

Your youngsters can sign, seal, and deliver the postcards made in this seasonal writing center. Stock a center with an assortment of writing utensils, scissors, used holiday greeting cards, and Christmas seals. To use this center, a child cuts off the front of a greeting card. He then turns the card front to the blank side, writes a message or draws a picture on the card, and "addresses" it. To finish the postcard, he places a Christmas seal in the top right corner to represent a stamp. All ready for a special hand delivery!

Susan Rau—Gr. K
Energy Child Development Center
Germantown, MD

Picture Cards

Picture cards promote writing practice. Glue pictures from old workbooks to five-inch sentence strip lengths. Using dashed letters, program each strip with the name of the picture. (Delete this programming if your youngsters have more advanced phonics skills and are spelling independently.) Laminate the strips for durability. Place them in a box along with several wipe-off markers. A youngster selects a strip, then traces or writes the letters to spell the name of the picture. When he's finished, each youngster wipes away his work with a damp sponge, leaving the strips ready for the next worker.

Sr. M. Henrietta
Villa Sacred Heart
Danville, PA

Class Directory

A class directory is a super center idea that remains a favorite all year long. To make each directory page, mount a child's photograph on a large index card. Then (with parental approval) print each child's name, address, and telephone number on the card. Bind the pages together between two laminated construction-paper covers. Place the class directory in a letter-writing center and encourage youngsters to write and address cards and letters to classmates.

Mary Lou Vogler—Gr. K
Port Monmouth Road School
Keansburg, NJ

Margherita DiBello
Rt. 8, Box 14
Whiteville, NC 20000
(919) 555-1234

Write A Letter

With the implementations of a letter-writing center, you are sure to see a rise in youngsters' desires to give as well as receive. Stock a learning center with a wide variety of paper, stationery, cards, promotional stamps, rubber stamps, stickers, envelopes, pens, pencils, markers, and crayons. (Parents are often willing to donate stacks of unwanted stationery supplies!) When a youngster visits this center, she may use the supplies to write/draw a letter or card to whomever she chooses. (You can use the directory made in "Class Directory" above as a model for youngsters when they address their letters.) When a letter is complete, a youngster slides it into a school-made mailbox. At a designated time each day, choose a child (or two) to be the mail carrier(s) and deliver the mail for the day. Be sure to occasionally slip in a letter or two from yourself—especially if you notice any youngsters who have not received mail.

Cathie Pesa
P.C. Bunn Elementary
Youngstown, OH

Dear Jodie,
I like your dress.

From,
Kristen

Flannelboard Listening Center

These individual flannelboards are ideal for a listening center with a tape and corresponding flannelboard cutouts. To make the flannelboard, glue a standard piece of felt to the front of a file folder. Tape together the front and back sides of the two short edges of the folder. Be sure to leave the long side open to form a pocket. Place an audio recording of a story and related felt-backed story cutouts in the pocket. At a listening center, a youngster removes the supplies from the pocket, then listens to the story as she manipulates the characters on her own flannelboard.

Ann Gudowski—Preschool and Gr. K
Turtle Rock Private School
Lake Forest, CA

Space-Saver Listening Center

This listening center is a real space-saver! Spray paint a wooden clothes-drying rack. Store read-along books and the companion tapes or records in Ziploc® bags. Hang bags from the upper rungs of the rack and headphones from the lower rungs. Set tape recorders and record players on carpet squares. Provide additional carpet squares for seating. Children listen to their selections and replace items when they are finished.

Jeanne Thomas—Gr. K–1
Dugspur Elementary School
Dugspur, VA

Popularity Counts

Count on this counting activity to be a hit with your little ones. As you introduce each new number, place several cotton balls, beans, pieces of pasta, kernels of popped corn, or Cheerios on a clean, Styrofoam® meat tray. Also provide markers, construction paper, and glue. To complete the activity, have each student write the numeral on his paper, select a corresponding number of objects from the meat tray, and glue them to his sheet of construction paper. Selecting and counting the items is a lot of learning fun!

Michele Melson—Gr. K
Cartersville, GA

Collecting Shells

Children can reinforce their counting skills while participating in a favorite summer activity—collecting shells. Program each of ten (or more) pages of a seashell notepad (or cutouts) with a different numeral. Place the programmed pages and a collection of shells in a center. To use this center, a child chooses a page, then places the indicated number of shells on or around that page. If desired, also have each child numerically sequence the pages.

Pat Johnson
United Methodist Preschool
Reynoldsburg, OH

French-Fried Counting

An order of these fries adds up to counting fun. Ask a local fast-food restaurant for a donation of french-fry boxes. Program each box with a different numeral. Make "fries" by cutting yellow sponges into strips. Place the boxes and fries in a center. To do this activity, a child places the appropriate number of fries in each box.

Lesa M. Whatley—Pre/K
Family Day Care
Auburn, GA

Watermelon Fun

Here's a juicy way to practice numeral recognition and counting. For each number that you would like to include in this center, make a watermelon slice by coloring the rim of half of a paper plate green, and the center section red or pink. Write a numeral on each watermelon slice. Provide a supply of dried black beans or spray paint another type of bean black. To use this center, a child chooses a slice of watermelon, reads the numeral, and then places that many seeds (beans) on the slice. As a child completes this center, have her help herself to a slice of real watermelon and count the seeds as she eats!

Jeanette Warwick—Pre-K
Berkley/Campostella Early Childhood Education Center
Norfolk, VA

 **COUNTING**

How Many People?

This easy-to-make center is perfect for reinforcing student counting and sequencing skills. From discarded magazines, cut full-length pictures of people. Mount the pictures on ten tagboard squares of equal size to represent the numerals "one" to "ten." Laminate the squares for durability before placing them at a center. A student counts the number of people shown on each square, then places the squares in sequential order. As a follow-up activity, have students cut and paste magazine pictures onto sheets of construction paper to represent each of the numerals from one to ten. Create individual counting booklets by stapling each student's pages together.

Barbara Boldt—Gr. K
St. Luke's Episcopal School
Fort Worth, TX

Number Jars

Reinforce numeral recognition, counting, sorting, and fine-motor skills all in one center! Label each of ten plastic jars and lids with a numeral from "one" to "ten." (Add additional labeled jars as desired.) From a large supply of counting manipulatives (such as beans, buttons, toy cars, and keys), partially fill each of the jars with the indicated number of each type of manipulative. To use this center, a youngster selects a number jar, opens the jar, and counts each set of manipulatives. (To keep all the manipulatives in a limited area, provide a mat to define a youngster's work space.)

Debra Hedtke—Gr. K
Weber-Hardin Elementary
Mathis, TX

Ghostly Counting

This grinning ghost provides great counting practice. Decorate a ghost cutout from page 88 with Halloween stickers. On the back, put one of each sticker displayed and program as shown. Laminate the cutout and provide a wipe-off marker. Students count stickers and write their answers on the back. Students could also add or subtract different sticker types.

Nancy Farlow—Pre-K/Kindergarten
St. Joseph, MO

Count And Order

Your little mathematicians can strengthen counting and number-order skills at this math center. Depict the numbers one through ten by placing the appropriate number of objects in each of ten Ziploc® plastic bags. Display the bags along with a supply of 4" x 6" paper at the center. A student places a piece of paper in front of each bag. He then counts and records the number of objects in each bag. Next he places the bags and papers in numerical order. As a finale, help the student staple his papers to make a number booklet, attaching a cover if desired. Extend the activity by having students illustrate their booklet pages.

Ann Higgins
St. Davids, Ontario
Canada

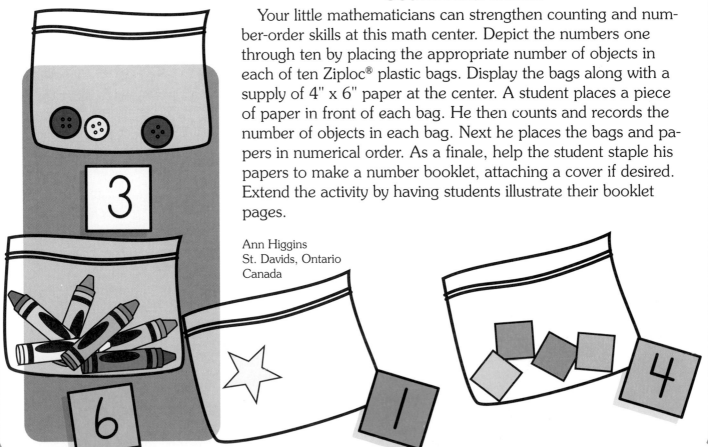

'Tis The Season To Count

Careful counters find success at this number-set center! Cut an even number of tree shapes (pattern page 89) from construction paper. Draw a matching number of ornaments on each cutout pair. For self-checking, label the back of matching cutouts with identical seasonal symbols such as candy canes, bells, or holly. Laminate the cutouts. Students match the cutouts by counting the ornaments, then flip the cutouts to check their counting skills.

Pots Of Gold

Your little ones will be only too eager to get their hands on this gold! Paint 11 small paper cups or nut cups black to resemble pots. Spray paint 55 (or more) beans gold. Label each of 11 shamrock cutouts from page 90 with a numeral from "zero" to "ten." Attach a labeled shamrock to each pot. To do this activity, a child puts the correct number of gold pieces in each pot. To extend the skills addressed at this center, you can have children put the shamrocks in numerical order. You can also spray paint some more beans and label a new set of shamrocks with simple addition or subtraction facts. Then attach these new shamrocks to the pots. Have children use the gold as counters and put gold pieces equivalent to the sums and differences in appropriate pots.

Susan J. Mills
Keswick Christian School
St. Petersburg, FL

Bears 'n' Bees

Youngsters' counting skills will be buzzing at this honey of a center! Using the patterns on page 91–92, duplicate ten bears and 55 bees onto construction paper. Laminate the cutouts for durability and cut out the patterns. Program the bear cutouts with the numerals "one" to "ten"; then code the backs with dot sets for self-checking. Store them in an empty, honey-flavored cereal box. A youngster selects a bear cutout, then places a matching number of bee cutouts on the honey pot. When his counting is complete, the youngster flips the bear cutout to check. It's a "grrreat" way to sweeten counting skills!

Debbie Johnson—Gr. K
Northside Elementary
Siloam Springs, AR

Dominoes

These oversized dominoes provide lots of math fun in a learning center. To make a domino, paint a block of wood black. When the paint is dry, put a strip of white adhesive tape on each side of the block to make the center lines. Drop a number of white paint dots onto each of the four resulting sections. Coat the entire domino with acrylic spray. During centers time, youngsters can use these easy-to-grip dominoes to play the traditional game or child-created games.

Lotto Fun

Use this version of the ever-popular lotto game at a small-group center and as a take-home game. Duplicate and cut out the gameboards on page 93 and the caller card patterns and parent letter on page 94. Place the gameboards and stacked caller cards at a center with a bowl of markers (such as beans, pennies, or squares of paper). To play, each child chooses a gameboard and eight markers. In turn, a child draws the top caller card and announces the numeral to be covered with a marker. When a child has covered all of the numerals on his gameboard, he calls out, "Lotto!"

To send the game home, store a set of caller cards and gameboards, a supply of markers, and the parent note in a zippered plastic bag.

Susan Osborn—Gr. K
Carrie Martin Elementary
Loveland, CO

Number "Stamp-ede"

This number-recognition center is certain to earn youngsters' stamp of approval. In advance, prepare a supply of blank forms similar to the ones shown. Place the forms in a center along with a stamp pad and a set of ministamps. A youngster selects a form and stamps designs inside the numeral outline. He then stamps a matching numeral freehand and stamps one design above each of the programmed numerals. Looks like a number "stamp-ede"!

Michelle Bourlet
Clayton, GA

MATCHING NUMERALS AND SETS

$$4 \overset{+2}{=}$$

Valentine Counting

Youngsters will take counting skills to heart while working at this center. Cut sentence strips in half to make cards. On each of the cards, place a different number of colorful valentine stickers. To correspond with each of the cards, glue a numbered heart cutout from page 95 to the closed end of a spring-type clothespin. A youngster selects a card, finds a "heartpin" with a corresponding numeral, then clips that heartpin to the card. If desired, program the backs of the cards for self-checking. Store all of the cards and heartpins in a string-tie envelope.

Count Around

Round out counting skills with this hands-on center! Glue pictures of sets of objects to represent the numbers "one" through "five" on a 20-inch poster-board circle. Use a marker to encircle each set; then laminate the circle. Program each of five milk jug lids with a different number from "one" to "five." Seal the lids in a Ziploc® bag. Punch a hole in the corner of the bag and another one near the edge of the circle. Attach the bag to the circle with a shower curtain ring. A youngster removes the milk jug lids, then places them atop the matching sets.

Betty Gomillion
South Leake Elementary School
Walnut Grove, MS

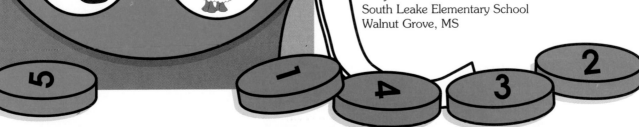

Outline Numbers

Your math center will be buzzing with activity when these outline numbers are introduced. Cut out the numerals one through ten from colored construction paper. Glue the center of each cutout (see illustration), then lay the cutout on another piece of construction paper. Make a variety of manipulative cards for students to sort and slip under the edges of the numbers. Store each set of cards in an envelope at the center. Manipulative card suggestions: word cards, number set cards, numeral cards, individual cutouts for each number (three pigs, five ducks, etc.).

Lois Putnam
Pilot Mountain, NC

Do not glue edges down.

Old Stamps

Your youngsters' math skills are sure to improve with this "send-off"! Make a slot (the width of an envelope) in the lid of a box; then decorate the box to resemble a mailbox. Cut used stamps from envelopes of old cards and letters. Glue sets of stamps onto different envelopes. On poster-board cards, write a numeral to match each of the stamp sets. Have a youngster insert a numeral card into the envelope with the corresponding set; then "mail" the envelope. Good work, Mr. Postman!

Sandra Hatton—Gr. K
Garth Elementary
Georgetown, KY

Barnyard Counting

Gather 'round for some counting fun with these barnyard buddies. To make the center, duplicate ten copies of the farmer and the animal pictures (page 97) onto tagboard. Duplicate ten *enlarged* copies of the barn pattern on page 96 onto red tagboard. Label each farmer's pail with a different numeral from "one" to "ten." Color the farmer and animals; then cut out the animal pictures. Glue the animals to the barns in sets of one through ten. Laminate all of the patterns and cut them out. To use this center, a youngster counts the animals on a barn cutout; then he matches it to a farmer with the matching numeral on his pail.

Liz Mooney—Gr. K
Central Rayne
Rayne, LA

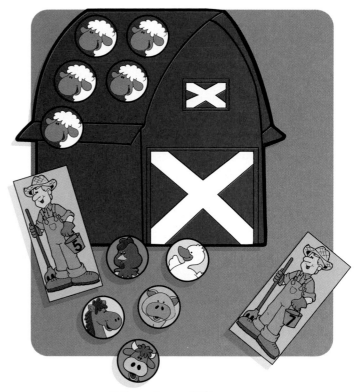

Number Flips

Fall into counting with number flips! Use tan construction paper to duplicate six copies of the squirrel pattern on page 98. Cut out one squirrel along the bold outline. From the remaining five copies, separately cut out the middle and bottom portions of the squirrel's body along the dotted lines. Pair middle and bottom portions. Using a different color of marker for each pair, program the bottom portion of a matching pair with a numeral from "one" to "five" and the middle portion with a corresponding set of acorns. Laminate all pieces for durability. In random order, stack the middle and bottom portions atop the uncut squirrel cutout. To make a number flip booklet, punch holes at the dots. Join the pages with small metal rings. To use this center, a child flips the middle and bottom portions of the squirrel's body to match, checking his answer by making sure both the number and the acorn set are the same color.

adapted from an idea by Andrea Bernard—Gr. K
Acadian Elementary
Houma, LA

Magnetic Math

Youngsters are sure to be attracted to this fun math center. Cover a coffee can with construction or Con-Tact® paper. Cut five leaf shapes from page 99 in fall colors of construction paper. Program each cutout with a different number from "one" to "five." Glue the leaves to the coffee can; then cover the can with clear Con-Tact® paper. Duplicate the acorn cutouts on page 99. Program the backs of the cutouts with corresponding numbers for self-checking. Laminate the cutouts; then attach a piece of magnetic tape to the back of each one. Store the acorn cutouts inside the can. To use this center, a youngster attaches each acorn cutout to the corresponding leaf, then flips it over to check.

Susie Fendley—Gr. K
Flowers School
Montgomery, AL

Seasonal Sets

Counting sets becomes a cinch at this seasonal center. Label a tongue depressor with a numeral. Enlarge a seasonal shape (such as the dreidel pattern—page 100) onto tagboard. Program the cutout with number sets, some which match the labeled depressor and some which do not. Punch a hole by each set. Staple a yarn length to a straw; then staple the yarn length to the depressor. Attach the depressor to the cutout. Code the back for self-checking. A student counts each set on the cutout. If he thinks the set matches the numeral on the tongue depressor, he places the straw in the hole alongside the set. He then turns over the cutout to check his answer.

Buzzin' Around

Your busy bees will be delighted to do a little buzzing around this number center. For each number you would like to include, photocopy the bee, flower, and stem patterns (page 101) on construction paper. Program each bee with a numeral, each flower with a number word, and each stem with dots. Laminate the patterns. To do this activity, a child matches the corresponding bees, flowers, and stems. Another option is to provide a large supply of blank construction-paper stems so that each child can color the correct number of dots on each stem or add construction-paper leaves to each stem.

Wilma Droegemueller—Gr. K and Preschool
Zion Lutheran School
Mt. Pulaski, IL

Custom Clay Mats

Design clay mats to reinforce a bevy of skills and, as an added benefit, strengthen little hands for fine-motor tasks. Divide a large sheet of construction paper into horizontal sections. Program the left-hand side of each of the sections, leaving a large space on the right-hand side for clay work; then laminate the mat. During February, for example, program the mat with number words. Have a youngster make clay hearts in the amount of each number word; then place the hearts on the mat next to the appropriate number word. Program additional mats to include matching a set to a numeral, making addition equations, patterning, or letter and number formation.

Debbie Wessels—Gr. K
West Salisbury Elementary
Sailsbury, MD

SEQUENCING

Get Your Turtles In A Row

Use this manipulative activity to reinforce the concept of "one more." Duplicate ten copies of the turtle pattern (page 79) on white construction paper. Color each turtle's head, legs, and tail; then color sections of the turtles' shells in increments of one. For example, the first turtle will have one colored section on his shell, the second turtle two colored sections, the third turtle three colored sections, and so on. Laminate and cut out each of the turtle patterns. To do this activity, a child sequences the turtle cutouts so that each turtle has one more colored section than the one before it.

Wilma Droegemueller—Gr. K and Preschool
Zion Lutheran School
Mt. Pulaski, IL

Clip the pumpkins to the patch in order.

Clip It!

This file-folder activity can be made to enhance any season of the year and to reinforce numeral sequencing. Draw or attach art to the far left and far right sides of the inside of a file folder. Laminate the folder. Cut a slit for each space that you would like to have in the activity. Slip one side of a paper clip into each of the slits. Secure each paper clip in place by taping the other side of the paper clip to the back of the folder. Write directions on the folder with a permanent marker. Draw, laminate, cut out, and program seasonal cards. Store the cards in a zippered plastic bag. To do this activity, a youngster clips the cards to the folder in numerical order.

Large, Small, And In Between

Youngsters will delight in helping you make this size seriation center. Gather clovers of various sizes and press each one between waxed-paper sheets using a warm iron. Cut the center from an index card to make a frame for each of the clovers. Tape a pressed clover to each card frame. Store the clover cards in a resealable bag decorated with a leprechaun sticker. To use the cards, have a student remove them from the bag and put them in order by size.

Kaye Sowell—Gr. K
Pelahatchie Elementary School
Pelahatchie, MS

Photos For Sequencing

Each time your class participates in a sequential activity (such as planting seeds, carving a pumpkin, etc.), take a snapshot of each stage. These photos make an excellent sequencing activity. Have children put the photos in order at a center. Since students are sequencing real events rather than made-up ones, the activity is simpler and more meaningful for them.

Heather Harrison
Scarborough, Ontario
Canada

Shake, Rattle, And Listen!

Try this auditory approach to sequencing practice. You will need ten empty 35 mm film containers. Place one unpopped popcorn kernel in the first container, two kernels in the second, and three in the third. Continue in this manner until all containers hold kernels. (The last container should hold ten unpopped kernels of popcorn.) Securely tape each snap-on lid in place. Program the bottoms of the containers for self-checking if desired; then place them in random order at a center. Each student gently shakes and listens to the contents of each container, then attempts to order the containers from the least to the most kernels held.

Sarah Simpson—Gr. K
Pinar Elementary
Orlando, FL

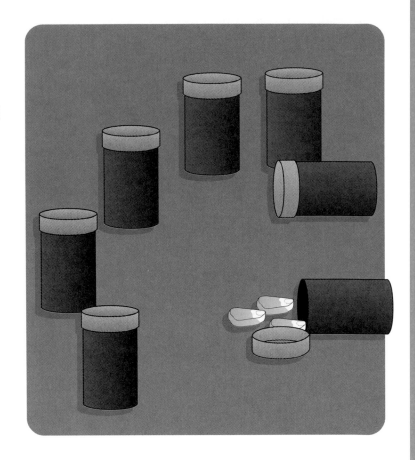

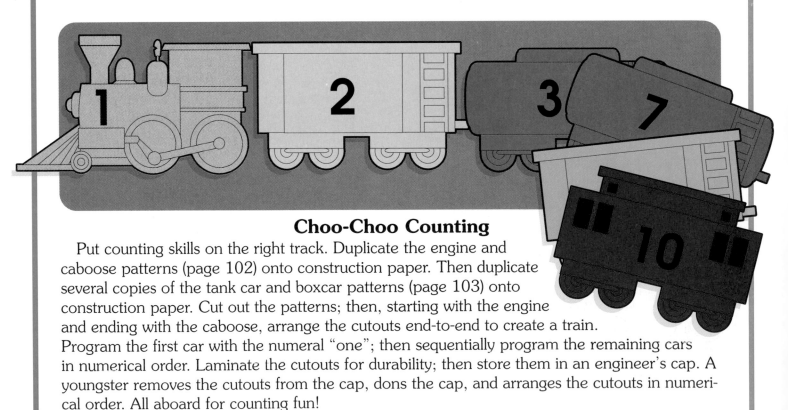

Choo-Choo Counting

Put counting skills on the right track. Duplicate the engine and caboose patterns (page 102) onto construction paper. Then duplicate several copies of the tank car and boxcar patterns (page 103) onto construction paper. Cut out the patterns; then, starting with the engine and ending with the caboose, arrange the cutouts end-to-end to create a train. Program the first car with the numeral "one"; then sequentially program the remaining cars in numerical order. Laminate the cutouts for durability; then store them in an engineer's cap. A youngster removes the cutouts from the cap, dons the cap, and arranges the cutouts in numerical order. All aboard for counting fun!

Debbie Johnson
Northside Elementary
Siloam Springs, AR

Pretty Patterns

Easter eggs lend a manipulative seasonal flair to this patterning center. Provide a basket of assorted colors of plastic eggs and a few empty egg cartons. Cut construction-paper egg shapes in colors that match your plastic eggs. Glue the egg shapes in various patterns onto tagboard cards. Have a youngster select a pattern card, then extend the pattern by placing plastic eggs in an egg carton. A youngster may also create an original pattern for a classmate to repeat or identify.

Kaye Sowell—Gr. K
Pelahatchie Elementary School
Pelahatchie, MS

Lid Patterning

Create a rainbow of colorful patterning activities using plastic lids from one-gallon jugs. Cut a set of 12" x 4" tagboard cards. Onto each card, repeatedly trace a plastic jug lid to form two rows of six circles. Color the circles in the *top* row of each card to create a pattern; then laminate the cards for durability. To create a storage container for this center activity, cut away the front portion of a one-gallon, plastic jug, leaving the handle intact. Store the cards in the plastic jug along with a collection of colored jug lids. To use this center, a youngster selects a card, then duplicates the colored pattern by placing a matching jug lid in the outline below each colored circle.

Jane Williams—Substitute Teacher
Louisville, OH

Patterning Paw Prints

Youngsters make tracks in patterning practice at this fun center. In advance, make paw-print stamps by carving a raised paw shape from a potato half. Or cut out and glue sponge pieces to a square of cardboard to resemble a paw print; then attach an empty spool to the cardboard for a handle. Place the paw-print stamps, construction paper, and several containers of different colors of paint in a center. Have students use the stamps and paints to create a variety of patterns.

Sheli Gossett
Avon Elementary
Avon Park, FL

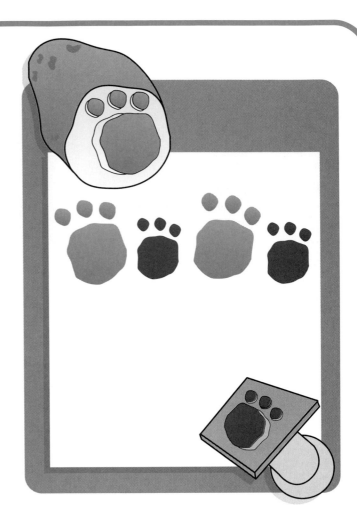

Pattern Tubes

These pattern tubes are just the right size for manipulating. Cut paper-towel tubes into a supply of three different lengths. Spray paint the longest lengths one color, the middle lengths another color, and the shortest lengths yet another color. Make pattern cards by drawing patterns that match the colors of the tubes. When the paint is dry, place the tubes and the pattern cards in a basket in a center. Have children duplicate the patterns that are on the cards and/or create their own patterns for a center partner to duplicate.

Dr. Sandra C. Richardson—Assistant Professor
Clinch Valley College
Wise, VA

Center Hookup

You'll be hooked on this versatile center format. Cover a three-foot section of a 2" x 4" wooden stud with Con-Tact® paper. At four-inch intervals, screw eight metal cup hooks into one side of the stud. Create a set of cards featuring patterns of colored shapes. Cut identical shapes from construction paper. Laminate them for durability; then punch a hole in each one. Punch a hole in the corner of a Ziploc® bag. Store the cutouts in the bag and hang it on one of the hooks. To use this center, a youngster places a card beside the stud, then hangs cutouts on the hooks to continue the pattern.

As a variation, program pairs of cutouts with numbers and number words, upper- and lowercase letters, or other skills. Hang one cutout from each pair on a different hook; then have youngsters hang each remaining cutout atop its match.

Linda Adams—Gr. K
Southside Christian School
Greenville, SC

Math Munchies

Munch and crunch your way through this fun-filled math activity. Stock your math center with four or five plastic bags, each filled with a different kind of cereal. Also provide laminated construction-paper strips. To use this center, a child takes several pieces of cereal from each bag; then he creates a pattern with the pieces on the construction-paper strip. To vary this activity, have him sort the cereal by color, shape, or size. When a child completes this center, allow him to munch on his cereal.

Kathy Grazko—Gr. K
St. Ann School
Cleveland Heights, OH

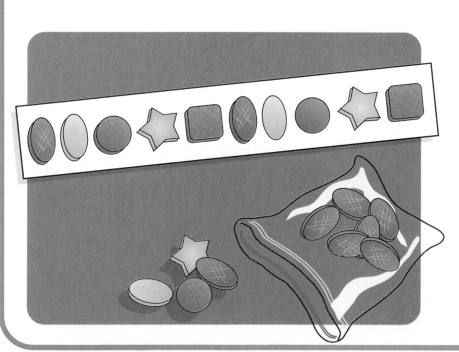

Sweet Graphing

Teachers beware: You'll have to hold *yourself* back from this center! Duplicate the graph on page 104. Fill a bowl with M&M's® and place a small drink-mix scoop near the bowl. Each youngster scoops one scoop of M&M's® onto a napkin and then places the M&M's® in neat rows in the appropriate columns on the graph. Next, he counts the M&M's® and records each total under the correct color word. Allow students to remove the M&M's® from the graph and munch on them while they color the number and color of M&M's® in each column. It's a treat that can't be beat!

Betty Lynn Scholtz—Gr. K
St. Ann's Catholic School
Charlotte, NC

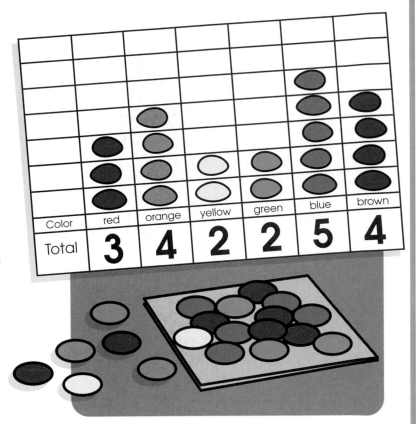

Color	red	orange	yellow	green	blue	brown
Total	3	4	2	2	5	4

Fruity Graph

This center provides a tasty way to pack a lot of learning into graphing fun. Duplicate the graph on page 105. For each child, provide a copy of the graph, a plastic bag containing about 15 pieces of Trix® fruit-shaped cereal, and crayons. To do this activity, a child takes one bag of cereal and a graph. As she removes each piece of cereal from her bag, she colors a space in the appropriate column of her graph, then eats the cereal piece. She continues to color and crunch until all of her cereal pieces are gone. Discuss with each child what her graph reveals, and/or discuss all of the graphs during a group time.

Mary Beth Brever—Gr. K
Rawson Elementary School
South Milwaukee, WI

banana	grapes	lime	orange	cherries

MEASUREMENT 4+2

Measurement Maneuvers

Size up measurement, counting, and number-writing skills at this manipulative center. Cut construction-paper strips (each of a different color) in various lengths. Place the strips, a supply of paper clips, buttons, or small cubes, and copies of an open answer sheet (similar to the one shown) at the center. A student colors the squares on his answer sheet to match the colored strips. He then measures the length of each strip by placing paper clips (or buttons or cubes) end to end. The student counts the clips, buttons, or cubes he used to measure each strip and records this number on his answer sheet next to the appropriately colored box.

Elke DuPree—Gr. K
Blackwell Elementary
Marietta, GA

Fossil Math

Transform your math center into a paleontologist's delight! Decorate the center area with toy dinosaurs. From white poster board, cut shapes of varying lengths and widths to represent bones or fossils. (Shape bones from sculptor's clay, if available, and let them dry for a week before using.) Provide rulers, counters, and tape measures for youngsters' use in measuring each bone. What a blast from the past!

Janet Paczak—Gr. K
Stevens Elementary
Brandon, MS

Spring Time

Put a little spring into telling time! Duplicate the clock face on page 106. Glue the faces atop tagboard flower cutouts from page 107. Then glue a tagboard stem and leaf to each cutout. Program each leaf with a different time; then program the back of each leaf for self-checking. Laminate the cutouts for durability. Use a brad to attach laminated clock hands to each cutout. Place them in a watering can at a center. A youngster removes the cutouts, then sets the hands on each one to match the programmed time. He then flips the cutout to check. What timely blossoms!

Lis Mooney—Gr. K
Central Rayne Elementary School
Rayne, LA

Around The Clock

Here's a center game to reinforce clock numeral placement. For each gameboard, glue a construction-paper clock to a colored background. Label each of several chips (in sets of 12 chips) with a numeral from 1 to 12. In turn, have each player roll a 12-sided die, then cover that numeral on his clock with the correctly labeled chip. If a player rolls a numeral that has already been covered with a chip, he passes the die to the next player. Continue playing until all the numerals on each clock are covered.

Elke DuPree—Gr. K
Shallowford Falls
Marietta, GA

Painting Center

Put a dab of color in your classroom with this neat painting center. Use a different color of paint to fill each of several empty glue-pen bottles with felt applicators. If glue-pen bottles are not available, use empty bingo marker bottles. Place the bottles and assorted paper in a center. When a youngster visits this center, he dabs the paint onto the paper to make the design or picture of his choice.

Patt Hall—Gr. K
Babson Park Elementary
Babson Park, FL

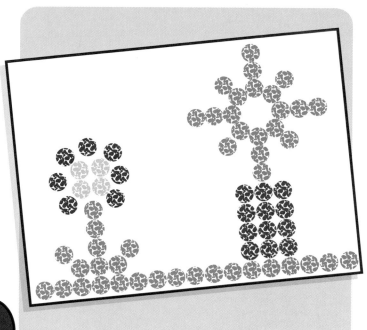

A Web Of Fun

Youngsters can create webs of their own while working at this fun art center. Using black fabric paint or colored glue, make four different webs on separate sheets of construction paper. Place the dried webs, white paper, and unwrapped crayons at the center. To use this center, a child chooses a web, then places the white paper atop the web to do a crayon rubbing. Have him complete the picture by drawing a spider, an egg sac, and/or spiderlings on the web.

Cathy Wiederhold—Gr. K
St. Peter The Apostle School
Savannah, GA

ARTS AND CRAFTS

Tub Toys

Youngsters can experiment with patterns while making these pretty pictures. Gather a collection of foam bathtub shapes (available in toy stores). Cover each of the bottoms of several shallow pans with a different color of paint. Have a youngster create patterns and/or pictures by lightly dipping a foam shape into a color of paint, then pressing the shape onto a piece of art paper. Repeat the process as often as he likes with the same or a different shape. Provide paintbrushes for adding details to the pictures.

Jeanette Anderson—Gr. K
James Leitch School
Fremont, CA

Picture Starters

Place a supply of picture starters in your art center and let the imagination begin! To make a picture starter, randomly place a sticker on a sheet of drawing paper. Stack a supply of picture starters in a center with crayons, markers, and/or paints. Encourage each youngster to choose a picture starter, then create a scene incorporating the sticker. If desired, vary the center by providing stickers and blank art paper so that each child can attach his sticker as he likes.

Christine Guanipa—Gr. K
Belmont, MA

Programmed Play Dough Mats

Play dough takes a new twist with specially programmed play dough mats. Using permanent markers or paint pens, program a set of solid-colored vinyl placemats with letters, numbers, or shapes. Place the mats in a center along with a supply of play dough. A youngster rolls out a small amount of play dough, places the roll on a programmed mat, and then bends the roll to form the letter, number, or shape.

Kim Ennis—Gr. K
Smiths Station Primary School
Smiths, AL

Homemade Play Dough

2 cups flour
1 cup salt
water

Stir flour and salt together.
Add just enough water to form a soft dough.
Store in an airtight container until needed.

Play Dough Decorations

Create "scent-sational" decorations from homemade play dough. Stock a center with a supply of seasonal cookie cutters, paint, paintbrushes, ribbon, and play dough which has had a few drops of a Christmas-scented oil (such as cinnamon or bayberry) added to it. At this creative center, a youngster rolls out the dough, then uses a cookie cutter to cut out a shape. He then punches a hole near the top of his shape with a pencil and sets it aside to dry. When his shape is dry, he paints it as desired. To complete each project, assist each youngster in tying a ribbon length through the hole. Display the completed projects on your classroom tree. It's beginning to look and *smell* a lot like Christmas!

Cindy Fischer
St. Mary's School
Bismarck, ND

Tracking Dinosaurs

The imaginations of your dinosaur enthusiasts are sure to roam about in this art center. Cut sponges into several sizes of dinosaur footprint shapes. Provide shallow bowls, each of which contains several paper towels that have been soaked with a color of paint. A child makes dinosaur footprints by dipping the sponge (dinosaur foot) into a color of paint and repeatedly pressing the sponge onto a piece of art paper. For added fun, provide a long sheet of butcher paper on which children can really "make tracks!"

Janet Paczak—Gr. K
Stevens Elementary
Brandon, MS

Thematic Art

Here's a tip to promote theme-related, creative art with a quick and easy cleanup. At your art center, provide one container stocked with supplies such as crayons, markers, scissors, glue, and hole punchers. For each theme unit, cover the outside of a cardboard soft-drink flat with bulletin-board border or adhesive covering. Stock each box with theme-related art materials such as collage supplies, tracers, illustrations, and literature. For example, you might have one box each for "Weather," "The Moon," and "America." After a youngster has worked at this center, cleanup is a breeze because he knows which box his supplies came from.

Mary Beth Heath—Gr. K
Murrells Inlet, SC

Pattern
Use with "Teddy Bear Twins" on page 12.

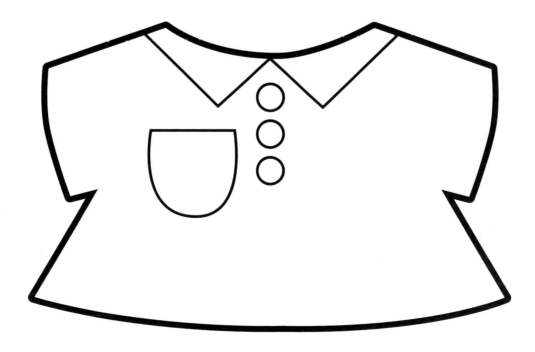

Patterns

Use with "Teddy Bear Twins" on page 12.

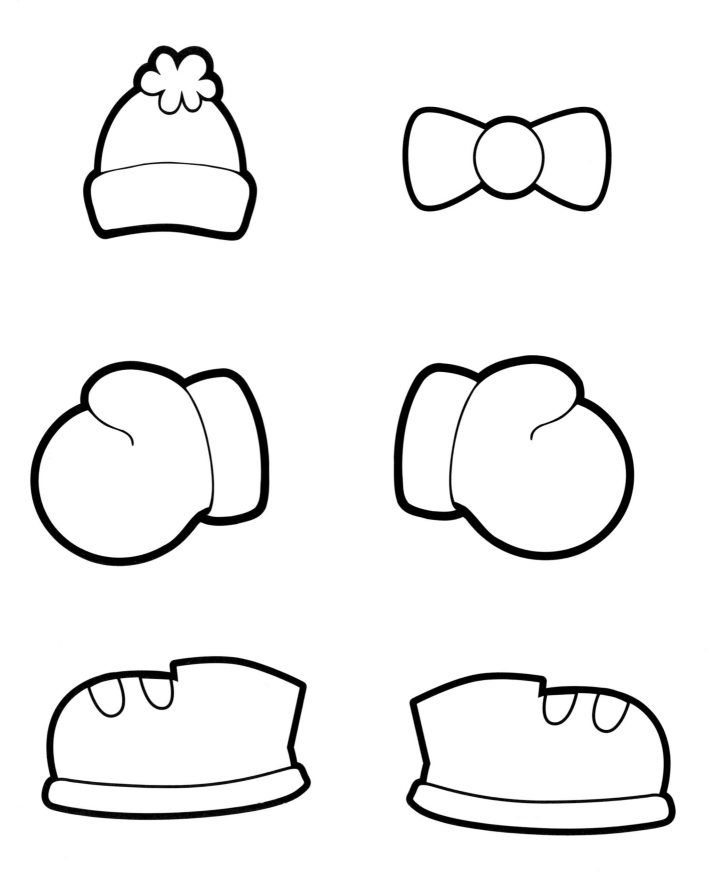

Pattern

Use with "A Spooky Match" on page 13.

Pattern
Use with "Turkey Shape Match" on page 16.

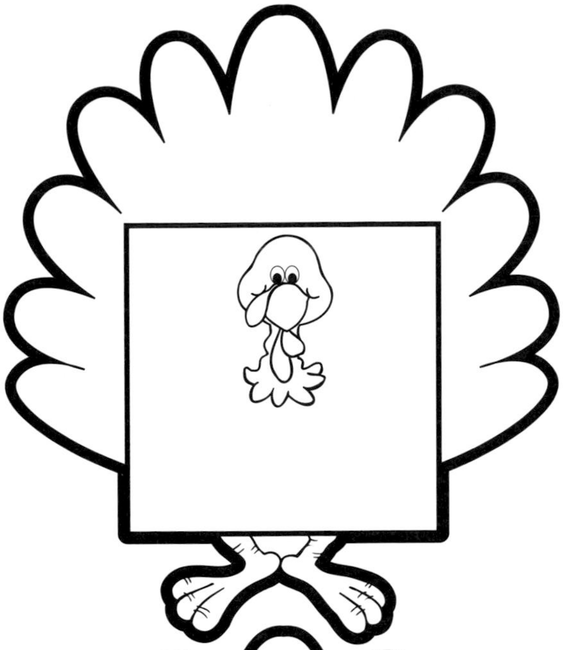

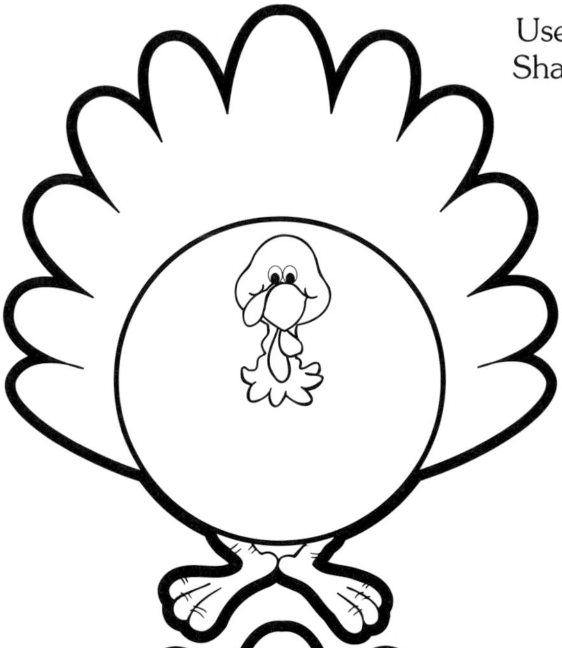

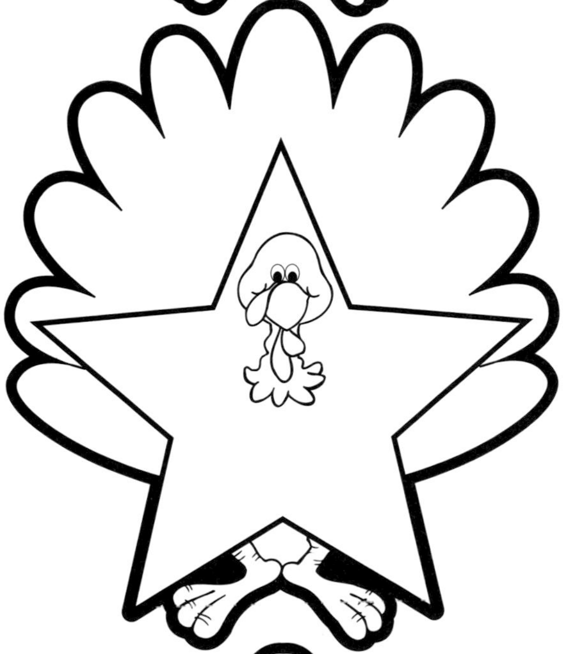

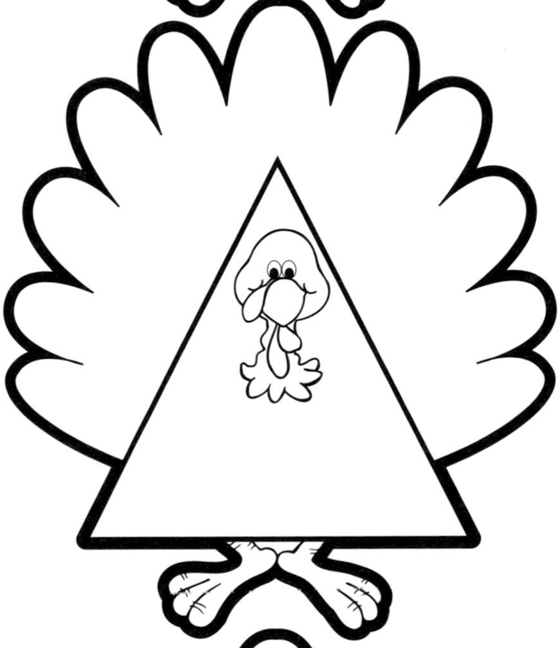

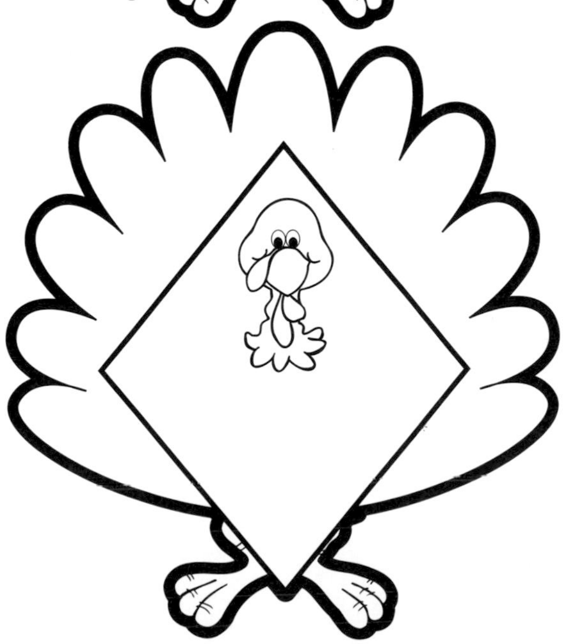

Snowflake Shapes

Match the shapes.

Note To Teacher: *Use with "Magic" Matching" on page 16.*

Patterns

Use with "Mama And Me" on page 28.

Pattern
Use with "The Friendly Ghost Castle" on page 29.

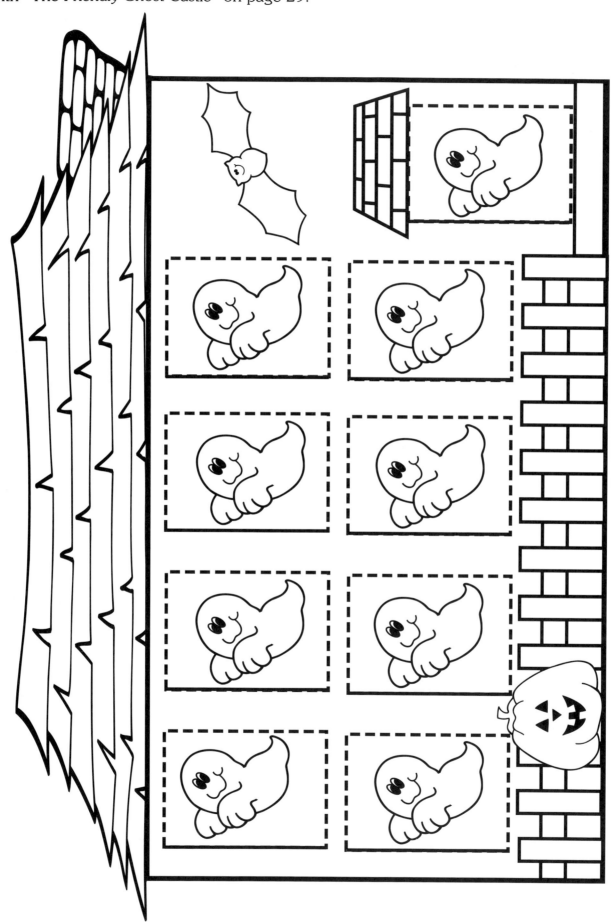

ghosts

Use with "Get Your Turtles In A Row" on page 54.

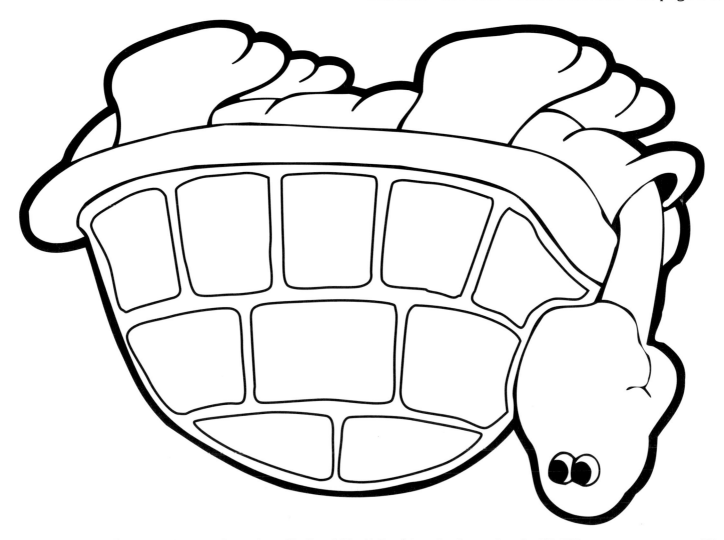

Pattern
Use with "Please, Feed The Monkey" on page 29.

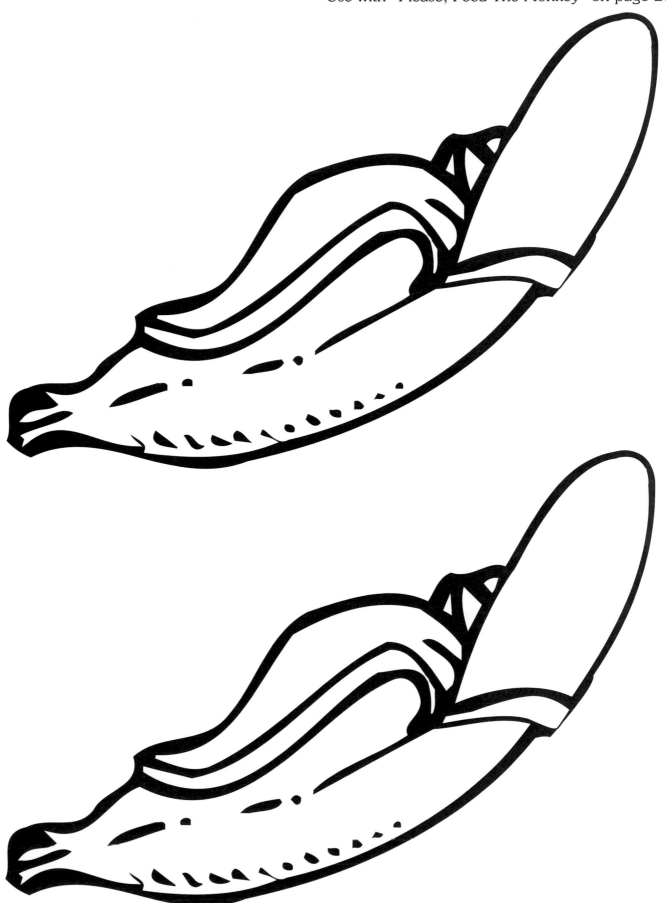

Pattern
Use with "Heart To Heart" on page 30.

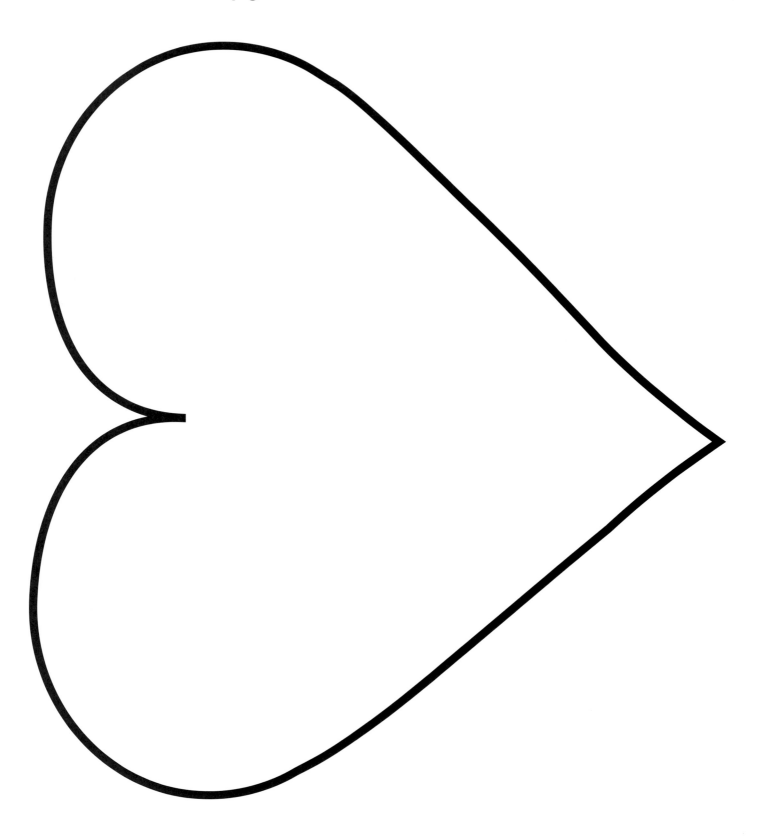

Use with "Catch 'n' Match" on page 31.

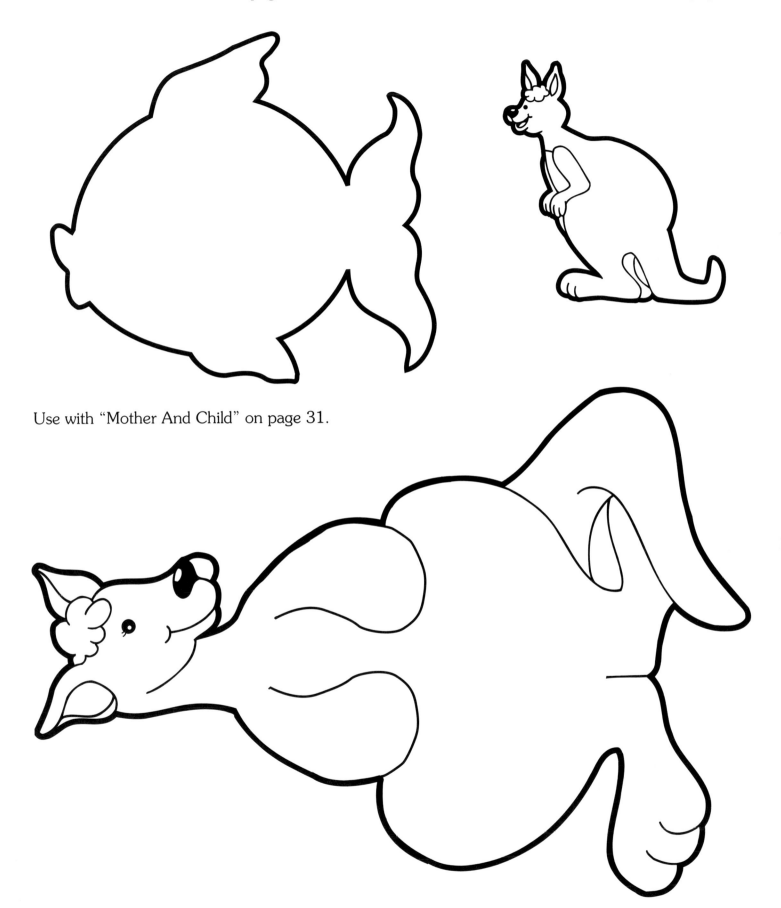

Use with "Mother And Child" on page 31.

Patterns

Use with "Shape Pads" on page 32.

Use "A Pretty Poinsettia" on with page 33.

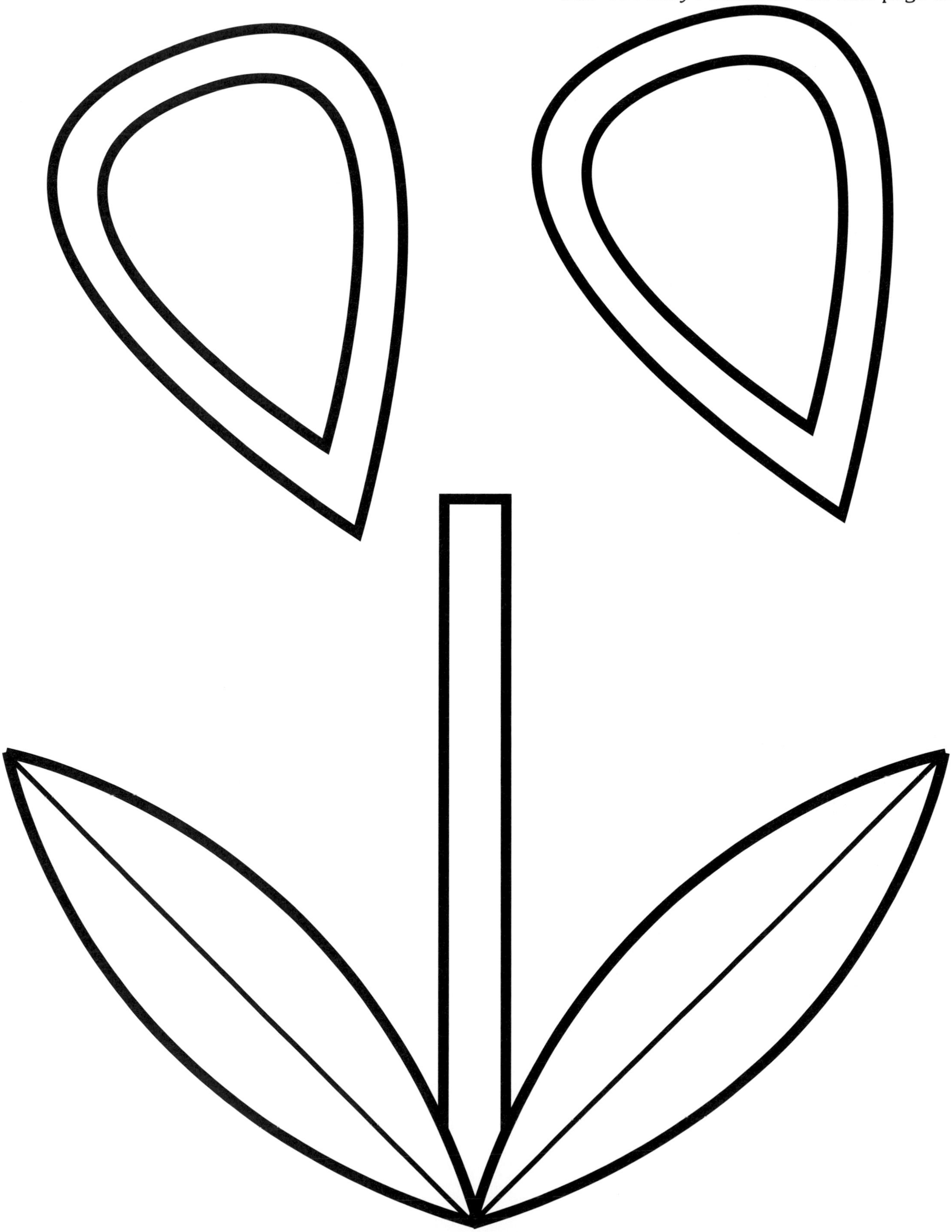

Patterns

Use with "Crowns And Castles" on page 35.

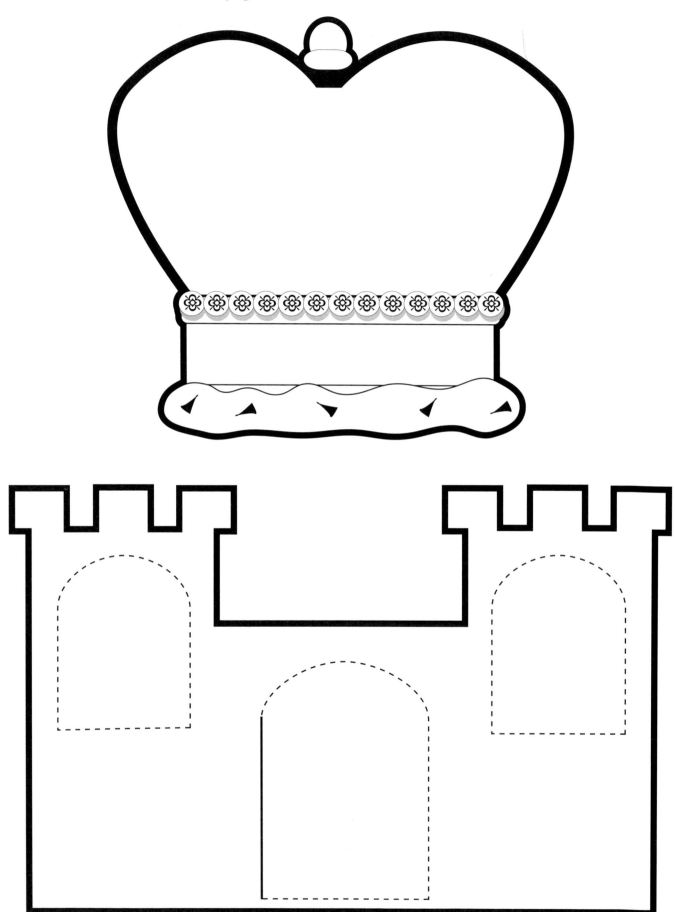

Pattern
Use with "Ghostly Counting" on page 45.

Pattern
Use with "Pots Of Gold" on page 46.

Pattern

Use with "Bears 'n' Bees" on page 47.

Lotto Fun

2	6	3	10
8	1	7	4

Lotto Fun

4	8	10	2
5	9	7	3

Lotto Fun

9	2	4	10
3	6	7	5

Lotto Fun

1	5	9	4
3	7	2	6

Pattern

Use with "Lotto Fun" on page 48.

Caller cards

1	2	3	4	5
6	7	8	9	10
1	2	3	4	5
6	7	8	9	10

Parent letter   Use with "Lotto Fun" on page 48.

Dear Parent,

We have been learning to recognize numerals from one to ten. You and your child can practice recognizing numerals at home with this numeral lotto game. To play, take all of the pieces out of the bag. Have your child give each player a gameboard and eight markers. Shuffle the caller cards; then choose one person to be the caller. Stack the caller cards facedown. The caller turns over the top caller card and announces the numeral. Any player who has that numeral on his gameboard marks that space with a marker. Continue playing in this manner. When a player has a marker on each of the spaces on his gameboard, he calls out, "Lotto!"

Have fun learning and playing!

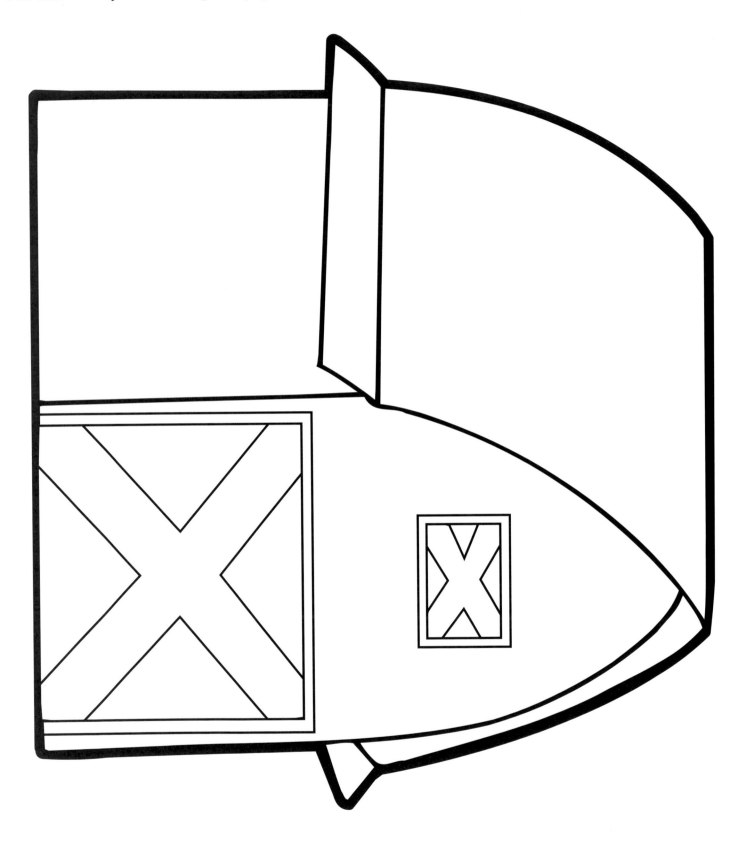

Pattern
Use with "Number Flips" on page 51.

Pattern
Use with "Seasonal Sets" on page 52.

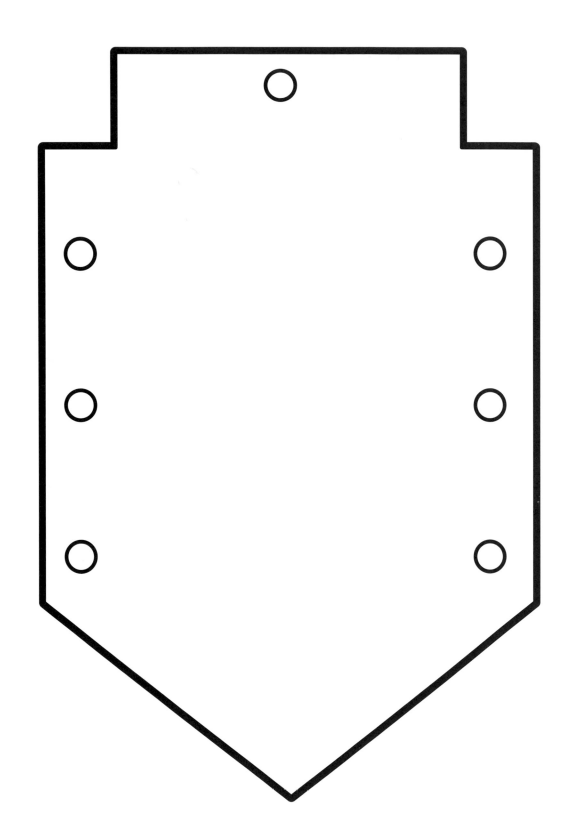

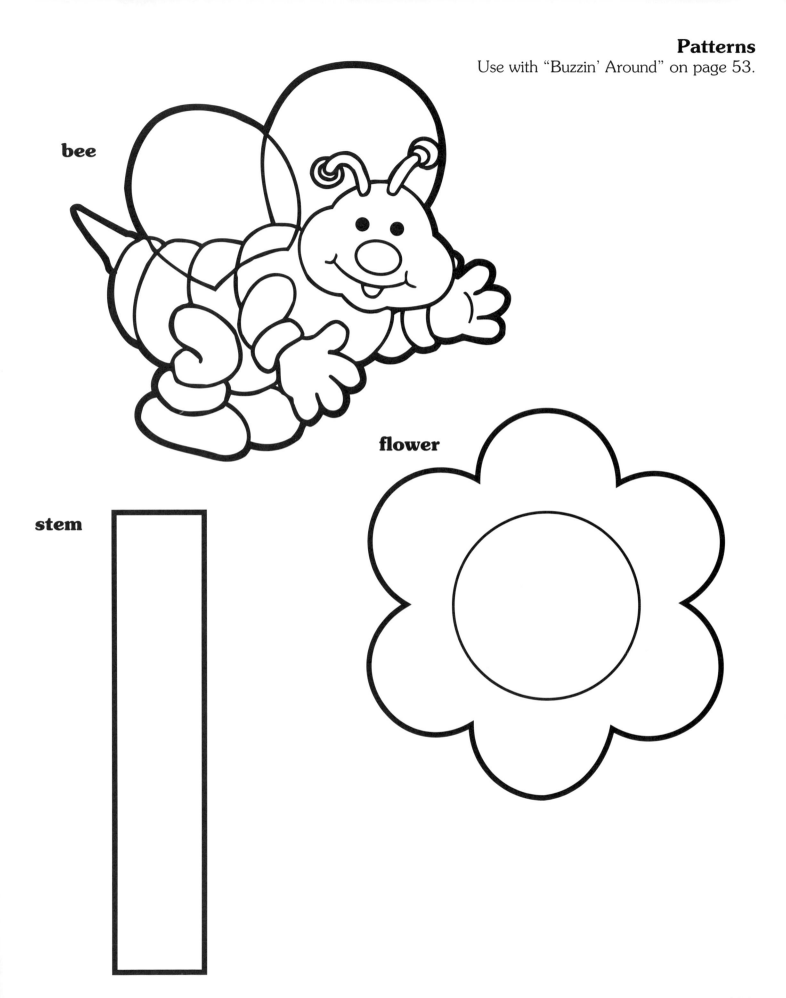

bee

flower

stem

Patterns

Use with "Choo-Choo Counting" on page 56.

engine

caboose

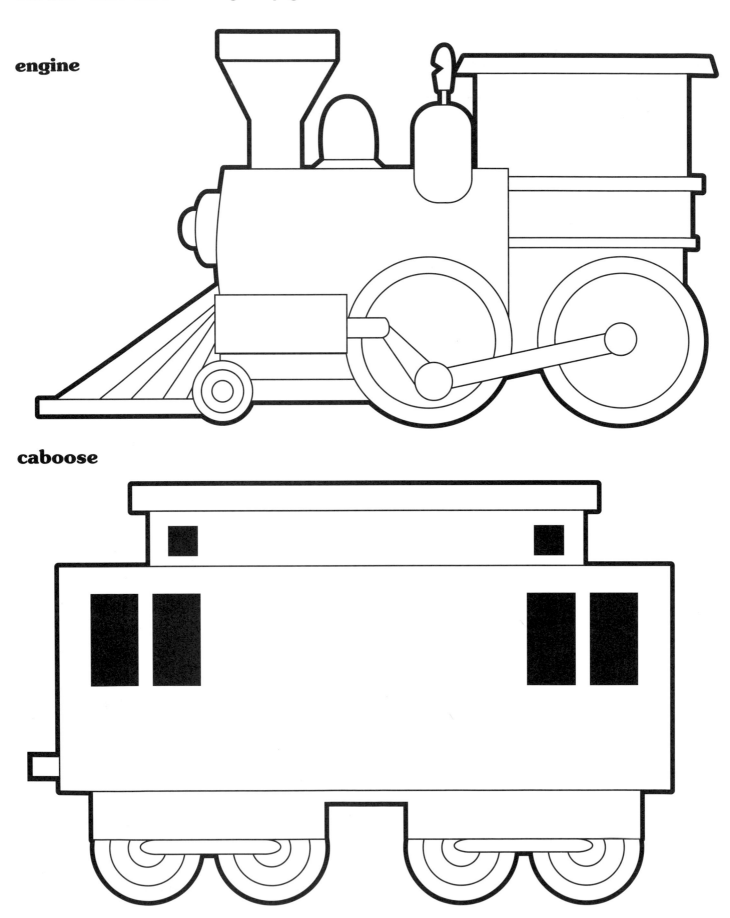

boxcar

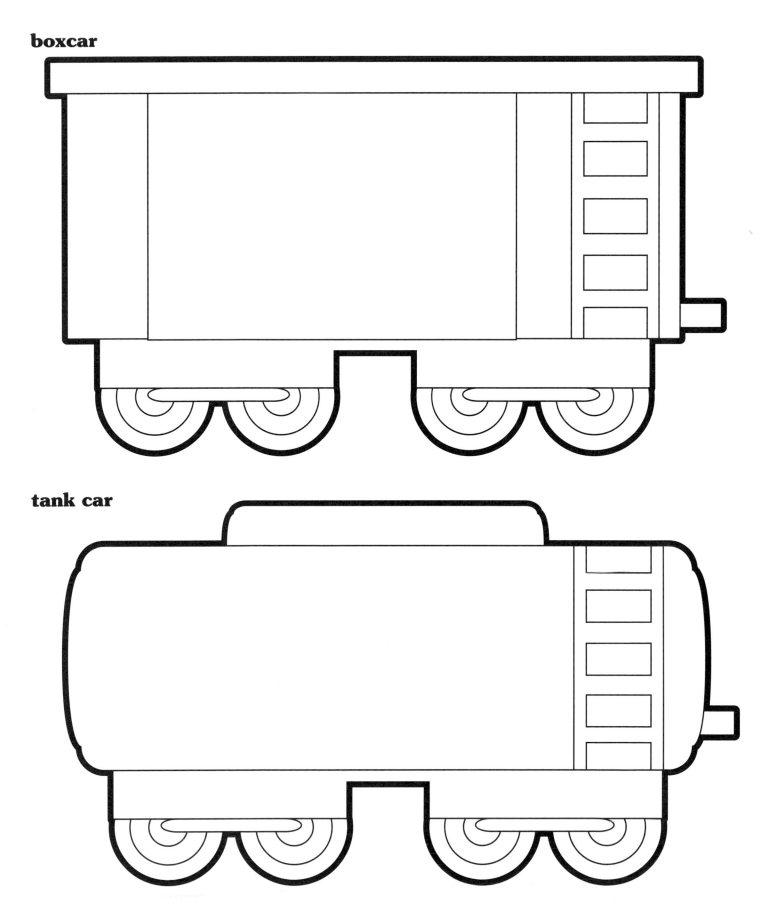

tank car

Total	Color							
	red							
	orange							
	yellow							
	green							
	blue							
	brown							

banana						
grapes						
lime						
orange						
cherries						

Pattern

Use with "Spring Time" on page 62.

Resource List
Rhyming

Initial Sounds

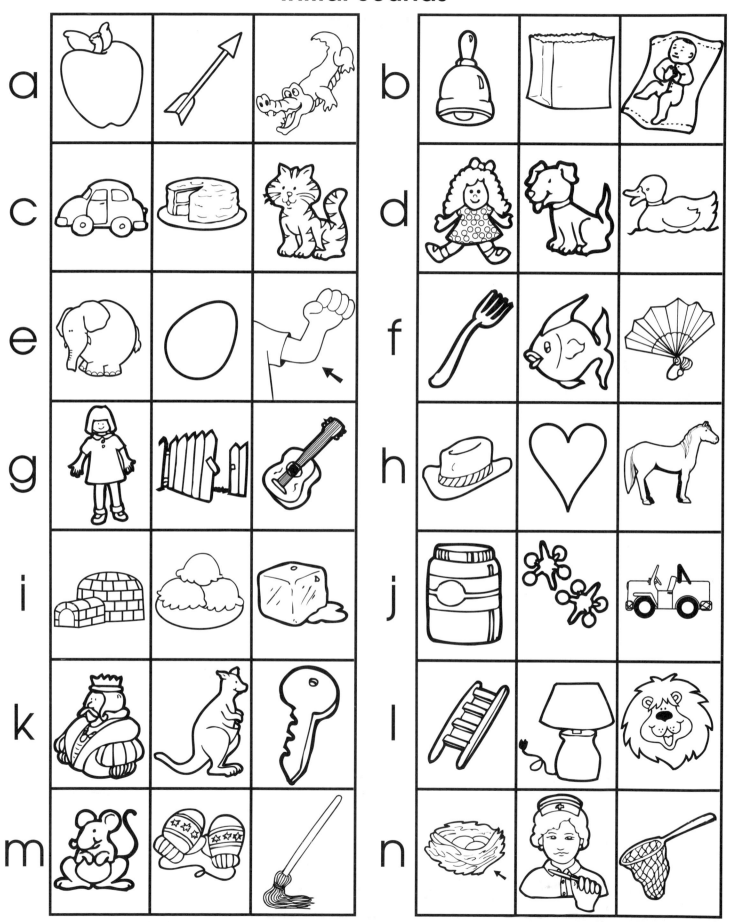

Initial Sounds

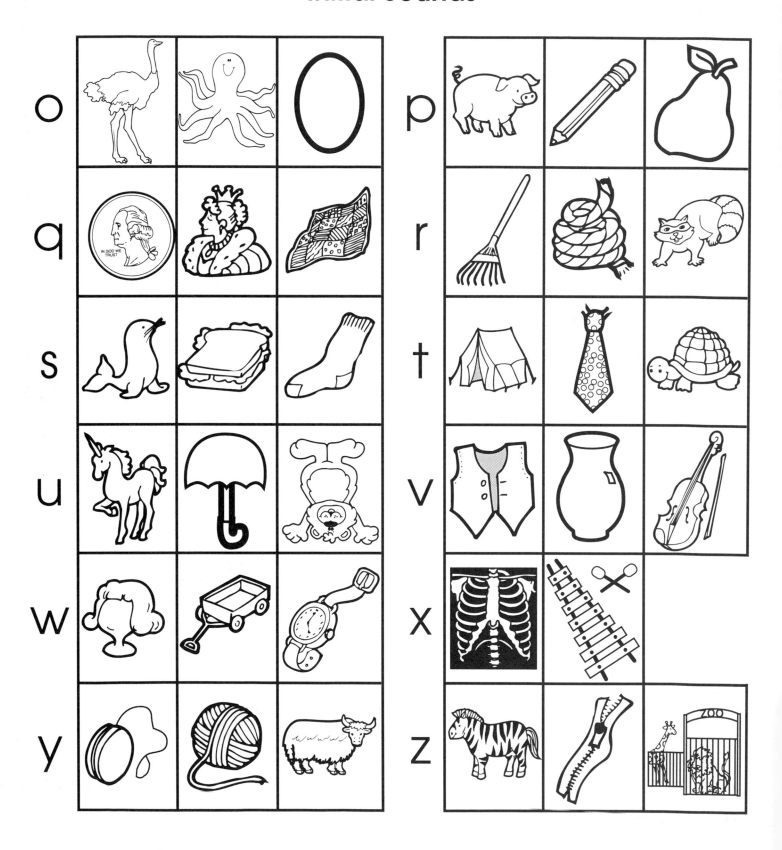

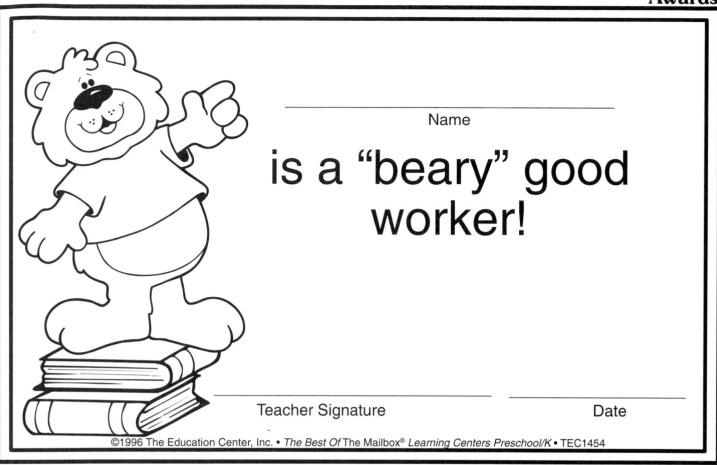

_____
Name

is a "beary" good worker!

_____   _____
Teacher Signature   Date

_____
Name

is a
Learning Center
STAR!

_____
Teacher Signature

_____
Date

Learning Center Stars

Name											